1992

Understanding UNIX
A Conceptual Guide
2nd Edition

James R. Groff
Paul N. Weinberg

W9-AEB-970

Que™ Corporation
Carmel, Indiana

Library of Congress Catalog No.: LC 88-60156
ISBN 0-88022-343-X

91 90 89   5

Interpretation of the printing code: the rightmost double-digit number is the year of the book's printing; the rightmost single-digit number, the number of the book's printing. For example, a printing code of 89-4 shows that the fourth printing of the book occurred in 1989.

About the Authors

James R. Groff

Jim Groff received a B.S. degree in mathematics from the Massachusetts Institute of Technology and an M.B.A. degree from Harvard University. He has published a number of technical articles on the UNIX system and UNIX networking in *Electronics, Systems and Software*, and *Mini-Micro Systems*. Mr. Groff is cofounder and president of Network Innovations Corporation, a developer of networking software that links PCs to data processing systems. Before starting Network Innovations, Mr. Groff was director of marketing at Plexus Computers, Inc., a leading UNIX system supplier. He has also held marketing positions at Hewlett-Packard, where he was responsible for the HP 100 series of personal computers.

Paul N. Weinberg

Paul Weinberg received a B.S. degree from the University of Michigan and an M.S. degree from Stanford University, both in computer science. He has held software development and marketing positions at Bell Laboratories, Hewlett-Packard, and Plexus Computers, Inc. Mr. Weinberg is cofounder and vice president of Network Innovations Corporation. His technical articles on UNIX software and performance measurement have appeared in *PC Magazine, Mini-Micro Systems*, and *Unique*. While at Stanford, Mr. Weinberg collaborated on *The Simple Solution to Rubik's Cube*, the best-selling book of 1981, with more than seven million copies in print.

Editorial Director
David F. Noble, Ph.D.

Acquisitions Editor
Terrie Lynn Solomon

Editor
Sandra Blackthorn

Production Foreman
Dennis Sheehan

Production
Dan Armstrong
Cindy L. Phipps
Joe Ramon
Mae Louise Shinault
Peter Tocco
Carrie L. Torres

Composed in Megaron
by Que Corporation

Table of Contents

Preface

Understanding UNIX, 2nd Edition, is designed to help you learn more about one of the most important trends in the computer industry—the steadily growing popularity of the UNIX operating system. The goal of this book is to provide a top-down, conceptual view of the UNIX system and its place in the world of computer software. This text is unlike the UNIX tutorials or UNIX introductions you may have considered buying or may already own. Our goal is not to provide a terminal aid for a new UNIX user, with step-by-step instructions on what to type next. Nor is our goal to make you a proficient C programmer using UNIX. Instead, this text presents an overall perspective of the UNIX system and the concepts that make it unique. In other words, this book seeks to answer the question: "What is UNIX, and why is it attracting so much attention?"

Understanding UNIX, 2nd Edition, is an appropriate text for anyone seeking technical or market insights into the UNIX system. The book can also be used as a college text in a computer science or business administration course. We assume that readers have some level of familiarity with computers and computer ideas. If you've used a personal computer, read a lot about computers, or come into contact with them at work, you should have no trouble understanding the concepts in this book. We specifically do not assume that you have had any prior experience with the UNIX system.

In some of the chapters in this book, the subject matter is explored at two different levels. These chapters are structured so that each one begins with a complete, high-level exposition of the topic. More advanced information is covered in later sections, each of which is marked with an asterisk to signify an *advanced topic*. You do not need to read these sections to obtain an understanding of what UNIX is and what it does. These sections present material that is important to computer professionals who need to know about the internal structure of the UNIX system.

Understanding UNIX, 2nd Edition, is organized topically. Chapter 1 introduces the UNIX system and presents its major features and their benefits. Chapter 2 provides an overview of UNIX's role as an emerging industry-standard operating system. This chapter includes the history and development of the UNIX system and compares UNIX to other standard microcomputer operating systems. Chapter 2 also discusses the different versions of UNIX and the UNIX standardization efforts.

The structure of the UNIX system is examined in Chapter 3. It identifies the major components of UNIX and explains their functions, benefits, and interrelationships.

One of the UNIX system's most powerful features is the UNIX file system, which is discussed in Chapter 4. This chapter describes the file system facilities for organizing and managing stored information, and for controlling system input and output. Chapter 5 describes the shell, the UNIX system's command interpreter. For many users the shell *is* UNIX, because it is the primary user interface for the UNIX system.

Chapters 6 and 7 discuss the features that make the UNIX operating system an excellent choice for multiuser computer systems. Chapter 6 examines multiuser operation from the user's perspective. And Chapter 7 covers the underlying structures that make UNIX an excellent foundation for building turnkey applications, where UNIX itself is invisible to the application user.

The next several chapters cover the four major areas in which UNIX offers a wealth of utility programs. Chapter 8 describes the utilities for file processing and data processing. UNIX tools that support text processing and office automation are covered in Chapter 9. UNIX has also earned an excellent reputation as a software development environment, and relevant tools for this application are described in Chapter 10. Chapter 11 outlines the UNIX utilities that support computer-to-computer communications and discusses the new emphasis on UNIX networking. The text includes descriptions of AT&T's Remote File sharing product and Sun MicroSystems Network File System.

Finally, Chapter 12 considers trends in the market for UNIX-based systems and software, as well as the future of UNIX itself. The market for UNIX-based systems and software is exploding. The market entry of AT&T and IBM makes it even more essential for you to understand the forces combining to create the UNIX phenomenon.

Conventions Used in this Book

Understanding UNIX, 2nd Edition, describes the features and utilities available with most versions of the UNIX system. The examples used throughout the book are applicable to UNIX System V. The text also describes XENIX, a popular microcomputer version of UNIX, and some of the more popular utilities from the Berkeley UNIX versions.

For readability, the names of programs, utilities, and files are set in **boldface type**. Computer prompts and responses are set in a `special type`, and user input is set in **boldface type**. When the contents of a file are reproduced in the text, they also appear in **boldface type**. Comments are included beside the appropriate line, on the right-hand side, following a pound sign (#).

Trademark Acknowledgments

Que Corporation has made every effort to supply trademark information about company names, products, and services mentioned in this book. Trademarks indicated below were derived from various sources. Que Corporation cannot attest to the accuracy of this information.

1-2-3 is a registered trademark of Lotus Development Corporation.

Altos is a registered trademark of Altos Computer Systems.

AT&T is a registered trademark of AT&T.

dBASE is a registered trademark of Ashton-Tate Company.

Eclipse is a trademark of Data General Corporation.

EtherNet is a trademark of 3Com Corporation.

GE 645 is a trademark of General Electric.

IBM is a registered trademark and OS/2 is a trademark of International Business Machines Corporation.

Macintosh is a trademark of Apple Computer, Inc.

MicroPro is a registered trademark of MicroPro International Corporation.

Motorola is a registered trademark of Motorola, Inc.

MS-DOS and XENIX are registered trademarks of Microsoft Corporation.

NCR Tower is a registered trademark of NCR Corporation.

NFS is a trademark of Sun Microsystems, Inc.

Onyx is a trademark of Onyx Systems.

PDP-7 and PDP-11 are trademarks and CP/M, DEC, and VAX are registered trademarks of Digital Equipment Corporation.

RADIO SHACK is a registered trademark of Radio Shack.

WordPerfect is a registered trademark of WordPerfect Corporation.

Z8000 is a trademark of Zilog, Inc.

CHAPTER

1

Introduction

The rapidly growing popularity and widespread acceptance of the UNIX™ operating system is one of the most important developments in the computer industry of the 1980s. From an obscure beginning at AT&T® Bell Laboratories in 1969, the UNIX system has become one of the most talked about and written about software packages ever developed. Articles on UNIX have become regular features in computer journals, and new UNIX-based systems are announced almost monthly. At last count, over a hundred different computer manufacturers offered UNIX-based systems, from personal computers to the largest supercomputers. UNIX is already a de facto standard in several segments of the computer market, and several standards bodies are working on official operating system standards based on UNIX. In short, UNIX has become a phenomenon.

Like any phenomenon, the UNIX system is controversial. UNIX advocates speak of its "elegance, power, and simplicity" and claim its superiority for a wide range of applications. Critics, on the other hand, charge that UNIX is "cryptic, unfriendly, and lacking in key features," and also unsuitable as a commercial operating system.

Exactly what is the UNIX system? Why do such intense interest and controversy surround it? How does UNIX relate to other computer operating systems, such as MS-DOS® and IBM®'s new OS/2™ operating system for personal computers? What are the relationships among the different versions of UNIX, such as System V, Berkeley UNIX, and XENIX®? What are the advantages of some of the well-known features of UNIX, such as its hierarchical file system, pipes, kernel, and shell? Finally, what is the role of UNIX in the computer marketplace of the late 1980s and 1990s?

Understanding UNIX, 2nd Edition, presents a conceptual overview of the UNIX system and its place in the computer industry. This book topically describes UNIX's main features and their benefits, with many easy-to-understand examples. *Understanding UNIX*, 2nd Edition, also relates the "UNIX phenomenon" to other trends in the development of microcomputer hardware and software. In summary, this book gives you the information you need to assess personally the significance of the UNIX system and its impact on you and your business.

The UNIX Operating System

UNIX is the name of a family of operating systems developed at Bell Laboratories. An *operating system* is the computer software that manages and controls the operation of a computer system. The operating system controls the computer hardware, manages system resources, runs programs in response to user commands, and supervises the interaction between the system and its users. The operating system also forms a foundation on which *applications software*—such as word-processing, spreadsheet, computer-aided design, and accounting programs—is developed and executed.

The operating system of a computer is largely responsible for determining its personality and usefulness. Depending on the design of the operating system, it may be particularly well-suited for certain applications and unsuited for others. The UNIX system is a general-purpose operating system, making it applicable to many different user environments.

UNIX has long enjoyed a reputation as an excellent software-development and document-processing environment and is widely used in these applications. The UNIX operating system is also especially popular in engineering and scientific applications. XENIX, a popular microcomputer version of UNIX, has been well accepted on multiuser microcomputer systems used by small businesses. Larger UNIX-based minicomputers also are used for commercial applications, such as accounting, inventory control, and order entry.

UNIX was not developed for real-time applications, although some UNIX versions have been modified extensively for these purposes. Despite the availability of UNIX on personal computers, the system has had small success in the personal computer market.

The UNIX Explosion

The market for computer systems and software based on the UNIX operating system has dramatically expanded during the last several years. As recently as the early 1980s, the UNIX system was available on only a handful of different computers. Most UNIX installations existed with the Bell system, where UNIX originated. Widely regarded as a tool for academic institutions and research labs, UNIX was far removed from the "real world" of commercial applications.

At this writing, more than a hundred different computer vendors offer UNIX-based systems. Several hundred other companies offer UNIX-based software, hardware, and services to extend the value of these computers. The market for UNIX-based systems, software, and services has grown to several billion dollars annually. UNIX is available on a broader range of computer systems than any other operating system.

At one end of the spectrum, UNIX is available on personal computers and even portable computers costing less than $3,000. Single-user versions of UNIX have turned these personal computers into powerful workstations for programmers. UNIX-based personal computers also have found a home in organizations where the computers are networked to larger UNIX-based systems. But UNIX continues to play a secondary role in this market segment, which is dominated by the MS-DOS operating system.

On larger microcomputers, UNIX is rapidly becoming the industry's standard multiuser operating system. At prices beginning well below $10,000, these "super microcomputers" offer performance that exceeds that of many minicomputers. The XENIX version of UNIX, from Microsoft, has had a major impact on multiuser small-business systems. The availability of XENIX on the IBM Personal Computer AT, the RADIO SHACK® computer family, and the Altos® computer series has made XENIX the most widely installed version of UNIX.

Perhaps the most important area where UNIX has achieved the status of a de facto standard is the market for engineering workstations. These powerful single-user systems are widely used for computer-aided design, manufacturing, software development, and other engineering applications. UNIX is the foundation of popular workstations from Sun Microsystems, Hewlett-Packard, Digital Equipment Corporation, and others; and UNIX is now available on Apple's Macintosh™ computers, making them attractive for computer-aided engineering applications. In response to market pressure for UNIX, other vendors now offer UNIX as an important alternative; one such vendor is Apollo Computers, who initially offered workstations based on proprietary operating systems.

UNIX has had a tremendous impact on the minicomputer market as well. Digital Equipment Corporation offers its own version of UNIX for the VAX® product line. Hewlett-Packard offers an entire family of UNIX-based systems, ranging from desktop systems to powerful super minicomputers. Other minicomputer vendors, including Data General, Prime, Wand, and Honeywell, also have introduced UNIX-based systems.

On larger systems, UNIX is available for mainframes from IBM and Amdahl. UNIX has become a standard operating system for the new generation of "mini-supercomputers," which are often used to solve complex engineering and statistical problems. UNIX is even available on the largest commercially available supercomputers from Cray Research.

Software Packages

The UNIX explosion also extends to UNIX-based software. More than a thousand different software packages are now available for use with UNIX—from language compilers to spreadsheet packages, and from word processors to database management systems, computer-aided engineering, and business applications. A few of these products are upgraded versions of simple personal computer packages. But the vast majority are powerful, sophisticated software packages originally designed for multiuser operation on minicomputers or for the high-resolution graphics of UNIX-based workstations. These products are now available on a much broader range of computer equipment because of the proliferation of UNIX.

Major UNIX Features and Benefits

UNIX is a comprehensive operating system with an amazing number of features and capabilities. Its major features (those responsible for its "claim to fame") are listed in Table 1.1. This set of features is cited by UNIX advocates as the reason why UNIX has emerged as the standard operating system for powerful 16-bit and 32-bit microcomputer systems.

Portability

The UNIX system is easily adapted to run on different computer systems. Moving UNIX to a new system typically requires only a few man-months of effort. As a result, UNIX has rapidly become available on a wide range of computer hardware. Customers can choose from over a hundred different

Table 1.1
Key Features of the UNIX System

- Portability
- Portable Applications Software
- Multiuser Operation
- Background Processing
- Hierarchical File System
- The UNIX Shell
- Pipes
- Utilities
- Text-Processing Tools
- Software Development Tools
- Maturity
- Enthusiastic User Community

hardware vendors, without being "locked in" to a single supplier. This *vendor independence* is a major benefit of the UNIX proliferation.

Portable Applications Software

Besides the UNIX system itself, the applications software written for UNIX is also portable. The same UNIX-based applications can run on micros, minis, and mainframes. Software suppliers can offer their software solutions on a broad spectrum of systems with different capacities and performances. Customers can choose the hardware and software combination that best meets their applications needs.

Multiuser Operation

UNIX is a multiuser system, designed to support a group of simultaneous users. The system allows efficient sharing of the processing power and the information storage of a computer system, while offering the security and protection features needed to insulate each user from the activities of other users. UNIX-based systems, with their ability to support many users working with common data and their low cost per user, are ideally suited for use in smaller businesses and departments of larger companies.

Background Processing

UNIX supports *background* processing, which allows a user to initiate a task and then proceed to other activities, while the system continues to work on the original task. For example, the system can be sorting a file and printing a report on a user's behalf at the same time that the user is editing a document. Background processing helps users to be more effective in using the system and in accomplishing more work in a given period of time.

Hierarchical File System

UNIX features a *hierarchical file system* for organizing stored information. The hierarchical structure offers maximum flexibility for grouping information in a way that reflects its natural structure. A single user's data, for example, may be grouped by activity. And data from many different users can be grouped according to corporate organization. As a result, stored data is easier to locate and to manage.

The UNIX Shell

User interaction with UNIX is controlled by the *shell*, a powerful command interpreter. The shell supports a number of convenient features, such as the ability to redirect application input and output, and the ability to manipulate groups of files with a single command. The shell also supports execution of predefined command sequences in conjunction with built-in programming language features. These capabilities allow even complex tasks to be performed by unsophisticated users.

Pipes

One of the most famous UNIX features is the *pipe*. Pipes are used to combine several simple programs to perform more complex functions. In many cases, new tasks require only that existing programs and utilities be combined using pipes, thus eliminating the need for new software development.

UNIX Utilities

UNIX includes over two hundred utility programs for functions like sorting data, processing text, and search for information. These utilities form a powerful collection of tools that can be used to accomplish many tasks without writing new programs.

Text-Processing Tools

UNIX offers a rich assortment of tools for all aspects of text processing. Text-editing utilities support the creation, editing, and management of documents. Text-formatting utilities generate output for a wide range of printing devices, from draft-quality printers to phototypesetters.

Software Development Tools

UNIX is widely recognized as an excellent system for software development. An extensive array of software tools supports all phases of the development process, from program editing through debugging. As a result, UNIX is widely used to develop systems and applications software for computers, from micros to mainframes.

Maturity

UNIX is a solid, time-tested operating system, which has been in use for over eighteen years. The software is mature and relatively free of bugs, offering a high level of reliability for an operating system of its capability.

User Community

Besides the technical advantages of UNIX, one of the main reasons for its success is the support of an enthusiastic user community. UNIX is widely used as a teaching tool, and each year colleges and universities produce a new crop of computer science graduates steeped in UNIX experience and tradition. Because of the popularity of UNIX on engineering and scientific computers, these engineers often continue to be enthusiastic UNIX users in their careers. The federal government, the Bell operating companies, and the high-technology industries also are heavy users of UNIX-based systems and have active user communities. Linked by an infrastructure of user groups, newsletters, magazines, and trade shows, these user communities have contributed to the demand for UNIX and UNIX-based software.

CHAPTER

2

A UNIX Perspective

T he UNIX system is often touted as a "de facto standard operating system." What does this mean? What advantages are offered by a standard? How can the UNIX system be a standard when there seem to be many different versions of it? And how did UNIX achieve its status of widespread acceptance and use? In examining the role of the UNIX system as an industry-standard operating system, this chapter provides answers to these questions.

Standards in the Computer Industry

The notion of a standard operating system is a relatively new one in the computer industry. In the 1970s the fastest growing part of the industry was comprised of minicomputer manufacturers, each offering nonstandard, proprietary products. While these manufacturers were developing their hardware and software products, each claimed the "best" processor, computer languages, and operating system. In choosing a vendor, a customer "locked himself in" to one manufacturer's gear since the costs of changing to another, incompatible system were prohibitive.

In contrast, the microcomputer era of the 1980s can be accurately called the "era of standards." True, there are hundreds of microcomputer systems available. But each is powered by one of a mere handful of standard microprocessors. Microcomputer peripherals are standardized around a handful of bus architectures and peripheral interfaces. Standard microcomputer operating systems have emerged as well.

Standard operating systems offer the following unique advantages to all participants in the microcomputer market:

- Customers benefit because they are no longer captive to a single manufacturer.

- Applications developers benefit because they can offer their software on a wide range of different systems.

- Computer manufacturers benefit from more rapid acceptance of their products and through reduced software development costs.

In fact, the development of standards may be the single largest contributor to the explosive growth of the microcomputer market.

CP/M—The First Standard Operating System

Any discussion of standard operating systems must begin with CP/M®, the first standard operating system for microcomputers. CP/M (Control Program for Microprocessors) was developed in the late 1970s for an early 8-bit microprocessor, the Intel 8080. Although the 8080 was popular from the start, software development for microcomputers was a tedious process in those days. Without the help of systems software, applications programs had to perform many low-level functions, such as input/output control, for themselves. Yet main memory was too precious to support the big operating systems that were typical of minicomputers.

Recognizing that the lack of systems was a barrier to rapid development of the market, early microcomputer manufacturers seized on CP/M when it was introduced by Digital Research. CP/M offered a good compromise operating system for the microcomputers of the day because of the following distinctions:

- It was small, requiring only about 8K of memory.

- It handled low-level input/output tasks, freeing programmers to concentrate on their applications.

- It was portable, with hardware-specific functions concentrated in one small part of the software.

- It was simple and easy to learn.

Adoption of CP/M by a few early microcomputer manufacturers set in motion the "standardization cycle" depicted in Figure 2.1. Availability of CP/M-based systems attracted software vendors to write CP/M-based applications. Availability of these applications meant that more customers could buy solutions to their word-processing and accounting problems, and other problems as well. Increased sales of systems attracted into the market more manufacturers who selected CP/M as their operating system. In a very short period of time, therefore, CP/M became the standard operating system for 8-bit microprocessors, with hundreds of computer systems and thousands of applications packages based on it.

MS-DOS—The Standard for 16-bit PCs

With CP/M firmly established as the dominant 8-bit operating system, the summer of 1981 produced a milestone event in the microcomputer market. IBM introduced the IBM PC, which had a 16-bit microprocessor, the Intel 8088. With this processor, the IBM PC leapfrogged the established market.

It is easy to forget how different the personal computer market of 1981 was from the market of today. Apple and Tandy, with their own proprietary operating systems, were the largest personal computer manufacturers. The other smaller manufacturers were clustered around CP/M. Of the major computer companies, only XEROX had introduced a personal computer product, and it too was based on CP/M. Hewlett-Packard had introduced its CP/M-based system the day before the IBM announcement.

At its announcement the IBM PC was long on hardware and very short on applications software. Three different operating systems were introduced to tap the widest range of existing software:

- *CP/M-86*, a 16-bit revision of CP/M which offered compatibility with 8-bit CP/M.

- The *UCSD Pascal p-system*, an interactive Pascal interpreter that offered excellent portability for applications software.

- *MS-DOS*, a brand new operating system written for IBM by Microsoft.

MS-DOS (Microsoft Disk Operating System) was the "sleeper" of the three systems, and, on the surface, it appeared the least likely to achieve dominant status. But with IBM's support and encouragement of third-party software

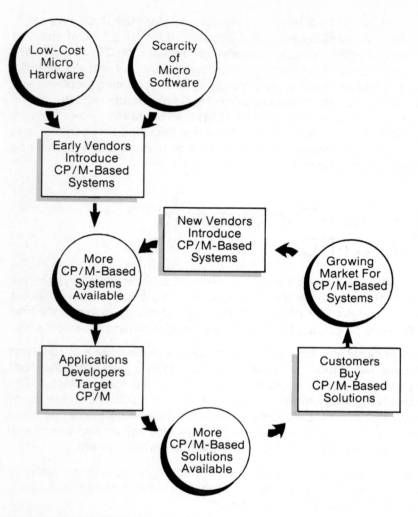

Fig. 2.1. *The Standardization Cycle*

developers, MS-DOS quickly vaulted into prominence as the standard operating system for the IBM PC. The standardization cycle was set in motion again for single-user 16-bit PCs, with a large "kick-start" from IBM. Again, the impact was dramatic. Manufacturers rushed to produce MS-DOS-based systems, and software suppliers created hundreds of MS-DOS-based software packages. The resulting PC market was measured in millions of units, compared to the tens of thousands for the earlier generation of 8-bit systems.

The Emergence of UNIX

The emergence of UNIX as a popular operating system is closely linked to the development of the new generation of 32-bit microprocessors, such as the Motorola® 68000 and the Intel 80286 and 80386. "Supermicro" systems based on these new processors offered computing power comparable to that of the minicomputers of only a few years earlier and opened up new applications for engineering workstations, software development, and small-business systems. With this dramatic improvement in hardware capability, computer hardware development again outpaced the industry's capacity to develop software for taking advantage of this increased capability. Once again, microcomputer manufacturers found themselves in a market starved for software.

At the same time, manufacturers of larger computer systems began to look closely at the explosion of the personal computer market based on the MS-DOS and IBM PC standard. The flurry of software development for MS-DOS systems created a proliferation of PC software that dwarfed the software available for proprietary multiuser systems. The focus of the creative energy in software shifted from proprietary minicomputers, which had been the fast-growing market in the 1970s, to personal computers. Thus, the success of the IBM PC awakened the rest of the computer market to the power of standards, and interest in a standard multiuser operating system began to build.

UNIX emerged to fill the role of a standard operating system for larger systems, playing the same role as that of CP/M and MS-DOS for earlier generations of personal computers. Because UNIX had been developed for minicomputers, it offered the level of sophistication needed to take advantage of 32-bit microprocessors and minicomputers. Specifically, UNIX provided multiuser support, excellent software development tools, features to support more powerful applications, and a file system capable of organizing and storing data in a multiuser environment. With the lessons of CP/M and MS-DOS still fresh, supermicro manufacturers rapidly seized on UNIX as their operating system of choice; and minicomputer vendors began to offer UNIX as an alternative to proprietary systems. At this writing, UNIX is offered on more multiuser computer systems than any other operating system, and new UNIX-based systems are still being introduced every month. The standardization cycle experienced by CP/M and MS-DOS is being replayed once more, with UNIX in the starring role.

The impact of UNIX, however, is being felt beyond its status as a standard for 32-bit microcomputers. UNIX occupies a unique role as the only single operating system that is portable across the entire range of personal computers, microcomputers, minicomputers, and mainframes. UNIX has attracted hundreds of hardware vendors and software vendors, who are creating literally thousands of applications packages. Portability then extends beyond UNIX itself to UNIX-based applications software. Figure 2.2 graphically illustrates this dual portability of UNIX.

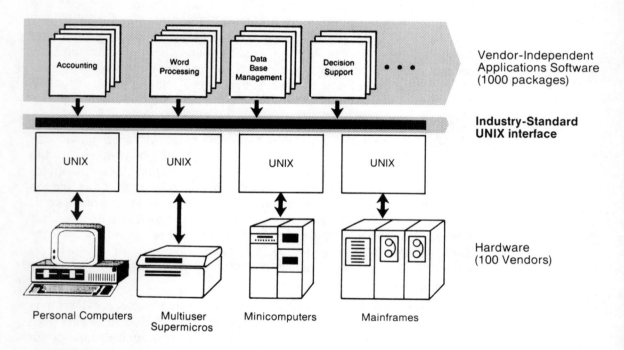

Fig. 2.2. *Portability of the UNIX System and Software*

Interesting comparisons can be made between UNIX and CP/M and MS-DOS, the earlier operating-system standards. Table 2.1 compares these three operating systems, providing several different measures of their relative sophistication. The larger size of the UNIX system and the number of UNIX commands and utilities available both demonstrate the power and capability of UNIX and its role on larger, more powerful systems. As the table shows, UNIX is not a rival standard to MS-DOS for personal computers. Rather, UNIX plays a *parallel* role to MS-DOS, as a standard for larger systems.

Table 2.1
An Operating System Comparison

Operating System	CP/M-80	MS-DOS 3.0	UNIX
Total System Software	Approx. 100 KBytes	Approx. 600 KBytes	Over 10 MBytes
Resident Operating System Size	8–12 KBytes	25–50 KBytes	100–500 KBytes
System Calls	Approx. 40	Approx. 75	Approx. 80
Commands & Utilities	Approx. 10	Approx. 50	Over 300
Typical System Price Range	$1,000–$5,000	$3,000–$10,000	$10,000–$200,000

A Brief UNIX History

For a system whose primary claim to fame is its sophisticated, multiuser features, the UNIX system had very humble origins. It not only began life as a single-user system, but also was a small, relatively unsophisticated piece of software, written for an obscure and long since obsolete computer system. Nonetheless, the creation of UNIX was unique in several respects. It was designed and developed by a small group of people with a single purpose in mind: to build a superior environment for software development. Unlike most commercial operating systems, which are developed "by committee" and designed to serve the proprietary needs of hardware manufacturers, UNIX was guided by a consistent vision of its purpose. Its developers also had a commitment to what computer scientists call "elegance"—a combination of simplicity, sophistication, power, and compactness. This guiding philosophy led to the development of an amazingly flexible and capable system.

The history of UNIX began in the late 1960s with a programmer named Ken Thompson, working at Bell Telephone Laboratories in New Jersey. Thompson and others in the Computing Science Research Group were using an early "time-sharing" computer, the General Electric GE 645™. The GE 645 ran an advanced, interactive operating system called Multics, which had been developed at MIT. Though the Multics system was powerful, it also was expensive to use, especially for one of Thompson's programs named Space Travel.

Thompson decided to move the Space Travel program to a dedicated computer system, a Digital Equipment Corporation PDP-7™. This system offered a good hardware environment for running Space Travel, but the computer lacked the kind of software support needed to develop programs like Thompson's. UNIX, then, was born out of necessity as a set of software routines to support use of the PDP-7. This first version of the UNIX system, completely written in PDP-7 assembly language, was completed in 1969.

The origin of the name "UNIX" carries its own irony. The name came from Multics, with the *multi*user orientation of that name changed to *uni* to reflect the single-user focus of UNIX. Multiuser versions of UNIX were to come much later, after it had been completely rewritten and transported to different hardware. The single-user version of UNIX became operational in 1971 and apparently caught on well within Bell Labs.

The early history of UNIX is closely intertwined with the development of the C programming language, in which later versions of the operating system were written. The original UNIX system was written in PDP-7 assembly language. A subsequent version incorporated software written in a language called "B," which was developed by Thompson in 1970. The B language was later used to help transport UNIX to the newer PDP-11™ family of systems in early 1971. The PDP-11 proved to be an extremely popular minicomputer system, both in the general marketplace and at Bell Labs. Groups within the Labs soon began using their PDP-11's with UNIX software instead of the proprietary DEC® operating systems.

The B language caught the eye of Dennis Ritchie, another programmer working at the Labs, who extended and refined the language, calling the result "C." The C language proved to be excellent for implementing system programs. It combined "structured programming" features, which have proved popular in languages like Pascal, with the ability to "get at the bits and bytes," which is required for efficiency in operating system development. The UNIX system itself was rewritten in C in 1973.

A major reason for rewriting UNIX in C was the desire to move UNIX to a wider range of machines. The first real test of UNIX portability came in mid-1977, with the decision to move UNIX to the Interdata 8/32, a 32-bit computer system very unlike the PDP-11. The Interdata port was successful, and UNIX has since been implemented on a wider range of hardware than any other operating system. Today, versions of UNIX System V are available from AT&T for the PDP-11 and VAX™ system families from DEC. Software houses and computer manufacturers outside AT&T have ported UNIX to an even broader variety of processors, from systems as small as the IBM PC to the multimillion-dollar Cray-II supercomputer.

Through the early and mid 1970s, UNIX remained primarily a tool for use within the Bell System, and AT&T discouraged its outside use through large license fees. Nonetheless, UNIX became popular among researchers doing work for the Department of Defense's Advanced Research Projects Agency (ARPA). Educational institutions were allowed to license UNIX at greatly reduced fees, and many universities took advantage of the opportunity. As a result, colleges became another UNIX stronghold. Today, over 80 percent of colleges granting degrees in computer science are licensed to use the UNIX system, and it is difficult for a computer science student to complete an undergraduate education without coming into contact with UNIX. Bell's liberal educational licensing policy has created a large pool of computer science graduates, all familiar with the advantages and capabilities of UNIX as a software development vehicle.

The history of UNIX as a commercially available operating system is a very short one. It began at a company named Onyx™ Systems, founded in 1978 by Bob Marsh and Kip Myers. The early Onyx systems were multiuser, 8-bit microcomputers, but attention soon turned to the more powerful 16-bit microprocessors. Convinced that 16-bit systems demanded a more powerful operating system than their 8-bit microcomputers, Marsh approached AT&T and successfully negotiated the first commercial UNIX license. An Onyx system running UNIX was shown at the National Computer Conference in 1980, much to the amazement of show attendees who couldn't believe that UNIX was actually running on a micro.

UNIX on microcomputers was given a further boost in late 1981 when AT&T announced new licensing provisions. Both royalty rates and the initial source code fee were reduced dramatically, and many licensing restrictions were relaxed. Today, a manufacturer can buy a version of UNIX for a newly introduced system for as little as $20,000 from a number of software companies who specialize in porting UNIX.

The most recent chapter in the history of UNIX began with the introduction of UNIX™ System V from AT&T in January, 1983. With the debut of System V, AT&T's position toward UNIX changed dramatically. Previous UNIX versions had been licensed as pieces of technology, but UNIX System V had the characteristics of a commercial operating system. Software support for UNIX was available for the first time, and the UNIX documentation was reorganized to provide tutorial materials separate from reference information. AT&T also announced that it was establishing UNIX System V as a standard and that future changes to UNIX would be upwardly compatible with the standard.

Since the introduction of UNIX System V, additional releases have appeared, introducing features important for commercial applications, such as spooling and file locking. AT&T itself entered the computer business with a family of systems based on UNIX System V. Thus, UNIX has made the transition from an early research project to a licensed technology and finally to a commercial operating system.

Versions of the UNIX System

One of the major attractions of UNIX has always been the ability to shape it to meet a variety of needs. During the early 1980s, this flexibility led to a proliferation of different versions of UNIX. In addition to several "official" AT&T versions, hardware manufacturers and software companies have adapted UNIX for various microcomputer systems. Because of deficiencies in the UNIX versions supplied by AT&T, these companies often introduced extensions to UNIX, further multiplying the number of versions. A few vendors, seeking the benefits of UNIX without the burden of AT&T license fees, developed UNIX look-alikes. These operating systems claimed compatibility with UNIX but were implemented from scratch without the benefit of AT&T's source code.

The UNIX system is available from AT&T in executable form only for AT&T computers and Digital Equipment's VAX systems. To make UNIX available on any other computer system, the system manufacturer purchases the UNIX source code and *ports* UNIX to its system. In this process, UNIX is adapted to work with the particular hardware features and input/output devices of the computer, and the user is insulated from these details. The vendor also may choose to enhance UNIX or to take advantage of unique hardware features to improve performance.

Another reason for the apparent diversity of UNIX versions is AT&T's policy toward licensing the UNIX brand name. AT&T licenses the UNIX software but not the UNIX trademark, which is retained for the company's exclusive use. Computer manufacturers, therefore, cannot name their ported versions UNIX. Instead, each vendor is forced to call the ported UNIX by a unique name, such as CTIX, HP-UX, or XENIX. These UNIX derivatives are generally compatible with one another. However, the proliferation of names has contributed even more to the confusion about multiple versions of UNIX.

Despite the apparent proliferation of UNIX versions, only three have had a major impact on the market: AT&T's versions, the Berkeley versions, and XENIX—a version of UNIX for Intel microprocessors developed by Microsoft.

AT&T Versions

Over a period of time, AT&T has licensed several successive versions of the UNIX system. Some of these versions were simply revisions of the system, whereas others added specialized features for a particular application. The major versions released by AT&T were the following:

- *Seventh Edition (Version 7)*: the first to be commercially licensed by AT&T. Most early microcomputer ports were based on Version 7.

- *PWB/UNIX (Programmer's Workbench)*: a specialized version that grew out of software development activity at the Bell Labs Business Information System Program (BISP). This version includes specialized utilities for managing software development by large teams of programmers. PWB/UNIX was initially installed inside Bell in late 1973 and was first licensed somewhat later.

- *UNIX SYSTEM III*: an update of Version 7, including the features of PWB/UNIX. System III was introduced in late 1981 and the following summer was first shipped on a microcomputer system by Plexus Computers, Inc. By late 1983 most microcomputer vendors had announced availability of System III for their systems.

- *UNIX SYSTEM V*: the latest version, announced in January, 1983. It includes performance improvements and enhanced process-to-process communications. System V marked the first time that AT&T licensed the version of UNIX currently in use within the Bell System.

Since 1983, AT&T has consolidated its efforts behind UNIX System V, and the earlier versions no longer play a major role in the UNIX market.

Berkeley UNIX

A great deal of UNIX development has taken place outside of Bell Labs. The University of California at Berkeley became a center of UNIX activity in the late 1970s, producing its own set of UNIX utilities and a UNIX port known as *Berkeley UNIX*, also called *4.1bsd* or *4.2bsd*, depending on the version. The Berkeley software includes support for virtual memory on the VAX superminicomputer family; a powerful text editor called **vi**; and a shell especially suited for C programming, called **csh** (the C-shell). Research attention also focused on file system performance and UNIX networking.

Berkeley UNIX became very popular not only in academic circles, but also in engineering and scientific applications, where the large address space offered by virtual memory is needed to accommodate large programs. AT&T has also recognized the value of the so called "Berkeley enhancements." System V contains many of the most popular ones.

XENIX

One of the best known versions of UNIX is the XENIX operating system from Microsoft. Microsoft has heavily promoted and advertised XENIX as an "improved" version for commercial use on microcomputer systems. It was derived from UNIX Version 7 and later, System III. Microsoft also has announced that it is working with AT&T on a version of XENIX that will be compatible with UNIX System V. XENIX's extensions to standard UNIX include file locking, interprocess communication, and various performance modifications for microcomputers. XENIX has been ported to the Intel 8086, Zilog Z8000™, and Motorola M68000™ microprocessor families.

Microsoft licenses XENIX to microcomputer systems manufacturers, who offer it as part of their product line. A new vendor of UNIX-based systems can thus purchase a XENIX port and avoid using its own engineering personnel to adapt UNIX to its particular hardware. Altos, Intel, and Tandy are the best known hardware manufacturers offering XENIX ports to date. The low prices and popularity of these systems have made XENIX the most widely installed version of UNIX.

UNIX Standardization

One of the main criticisms of UNIX in the mid-1980s was the lack of a single standard version. Unlike CP/M or MS-DOS, each of which is controlled by a single operating-system vendor, control over UNIX was spread among AT&T, the hardware vendors, and the UNIX software companies. The lack of a single standard had its most serious impact on the efforts of UNIX software developers. Although the various versions of UNIX were broadly compatible, their minor differences meant that applications software had to be slightly customized for each different version.

In 1981, /usr/group, an association of UNIX users and vendors, decided to address the lack of a standard. A committee formed by /usr/group began work on a written standard for UNIX-compatible systems. Participation in the effort came from leading UNIX-based hardware and software vendors and from AT&T. The resulting /usr/group standard was published in 1983 and was formally adopted in 1984.

In the meantime, AT&T began to realize the value of UNIX standardization. With the introduction of UNIX System V in 1983, AT&T announced that it considered System V the standard version of UNIX. Future versions of UNIX would build on the System V standard as upwardly compatible releases. This strategy was in marked contrast to the discontinuities that had characterized previous AT&T releases of UNIX.

To formalize the System V standard, AT&T published the *System V Interface Definition* (SVID), which specified the features of UNIX that were "guaranteed" to remain unchanged in future releases. SVID served two purposes. First, it was a benchmark against which other versions of UNIX could be measured to gauge their compatibility to the System V standard. Second, SVID was a foundation for building UNIX applications software. If applications software used only the operating-system functions specified in SVID, the software was guaranteed to be compatible with future AT&T UNIX versions and with other UNIX versions that were SVID-compatible.

As a companion to SVID, AT&T developed the *System V Verification Suite* (SVVS). SVVS is a family of programs that test the compatibility of an operating system with the *System V Interface Definition*. Thus, AT&T not only put forth System V as a standard but also gave the UNIX community a tool for testing an operating system's compatibility with that standard.

The evolution of System V since its introduction has delivered the promised standardization. New System V releases have provided additional features and functions but have maintained upward compatibility with earlier versions. The *System V Interface Document* has grown to three volumes and includes specifications of new System V features as extensions to the standard. The *System V Verification Suite* has been updated to test these extensions.

More importantly, AT&T has taken action to bring the other major UNIX versions into line with the System V standard. AT&T and Sun Microsystems have announced that they are working to address the remaining incompatibilities between the Berkeley version and System V, with the goal of producing a single merged version of UNIX. Sun plays a key role in the evolution of the Berkeley UNIX version because many Berkeley developers now are Sun employees, and Sun workstations represent the largest installed base of the Berkeley UNIX version.

In early 1987, AT&T and Microsoft announced a similar strategy for XENIX. The result of the AT&T-Microsoft alliance will be a new version of XENIX that is compatible with SVID and so will bring XENIX into the System V fold. In a break with past practice, AT&T is allowing Microsoft to use the UNIX brand name for this new XENIX version.

These announcements of compatibility plans clearly point to the emergence of UNIX System V as the de facto standard version of UNIX. Whether the development work toward merged versions bears fruit or whether the alternate versions slowly fade away is an open question at this writing. But the trend in the UNIX market clearly has reversed itself from the proliferation of UNIX versions in the early 1980s to convergence on UNIX System V.

Formal UNIX Standards

In parallel with AT&T's efforts to standardize the UNIX market on UNIX System V, several national and international standards groups have been working on formal specifications and standards for UNIX. The early standards work by /usr/group resulted in the formation of IEEE 1003.1, a formal IEEE standards committee. The goal of the committee was to develop a formal IEEE standard for a portable operating system. The committee published its standard *1003.1 Portable Operating System Standard for Computer Environments* (usually referred to as POSIX) in April, 1986. The 1003.1 standard, which focuses on the UNIX kernel, seems assured of adoption in 1987. Parallel IEEE committees are at work on standards for the user interface (shell) and UNIX tools (1003.2) and on development of validation tests to check adherence to the standards (1003.3).

The American National Standards Institute (ANSI) has established a committee to develop a standard for the C programming language. The standards for FORTRAN and COBOL developed by early ANSI committees have created a high degree of portability for those languages, and the goal of C language standardization was to establish this same portability for C. At this writing, the ANSI XJ311 committee has published its C language standard, which seems destined for approval.

Another organization involved in UNIX standardization is X/OPEN, an international consortium of computer manufacturers. X/OPEN's goal is to define an application-execution environment for software portability. The *X/OPEN Portability Guide* defines standards for the operating system environment, C and COBOL languages, commands, file management, database management, and internationalization. In January, 1987, X/OPEN announced that future versions of its *Portability Guide* would be based on the IEEE POSIX standard. X/OPEN has a strong influence over UNIX development in Europe. Most of the leading European computer manufacturers are members, including Bull, Ericsson, ICL, Olivetti, Nixdorf, Phillips, and Siemens. Other members are U.S. computer manufacturers with a strong European presence, including AT&T, DEC, HP, and Unisys.

Finally, the International Standards Organization (ISO) has also been active in UNIX and C standardization. The ISO effort has closely tracked the IEEE and ANSI committees and is on a similar time schedule. ISO should produce international standards for UNIX and C that are identical to the IEEE and ANSI versions.

The cooperative efforts of these formal standards organizations, along with AT&T's support of a System V standard, should provide continued convergence toward a common portable UNIX standard.

XENIX, OS/2, and the 80386

During the last several years, UNIX has had the strongest impact in the market for entry-level multiuser computer systems. Microsoft's XENIX has become the standard UNIX version for these systems, which are usually based on the Intel 8086 processor family. Due largely to the success of 80286-based systems from Altos and Tandy and a dedicated following on the IBM PC AT, XENIX has the largest installed base of any UNIX version.

With the introduction of the Intel 80386 microprocessor, XENIX-based multiuser systems are more powerful and more important. Because of the higher performance of the 80386, XENIX-based systems that typically cost under $20,000 are given the processing power of proprietary minicomputers costing well over $100,000. Further, the 80386 provides hardware support for multiuser features that XENIX was forced to perform in software on earlier 80286-based machines. In the fall of 1987, the first new version of XENIX taking advantage of the 80386 was announced by Santa Cruz Operation, one of Microsoft's XENIX development partners, for use on 20-megahertz, 80386-based systems from COMPAQ. As XENIX continues to take advantage of the 80386, and as even higher-performance 80386 chips become available, the price/performance advantage of XENIX-based systems will become even more pronounced.

Microsoft and AT&T also boosted the importance of XENIX by making announcements in early 1987 about its future evolution. Joint development work between the two companies will produce a future version of XENIX (XENIX System V) that is fully compatible with AT&T's System V Interface Document (SVID). Reversing its past stand, AT&T will allow Microsoft to market this future XENIX version under the UNIX trade name. Thus, over time, XENIX will lose its identity as a unique version of UNIX and become part of the UNIX System V mainstream.

With the announcement of a System V-compatible XENIX, Microsoft's strategy for XENIX has come full circle. Development of XENIX at Microsoft began even before the introduction of Microsoft's MS-DOS for the IBM PC. The original XENIX strategy was to offer the first commercially viable microcomputer version of UNIX and thus to establish XENIX as a unique, independent industry standard.

This original strategy consisted of four key elements:

- *Availability.* UNIX was available from AT&T only in the form of source code for Digital Equipment Corporation minicomputers. XENIX, on the other hand, was already configured and performance-tuned for use on microprocessors, significantly reducing the porting effort.

- *Commercial extensions.* XENIX included key features that were lacking in the UNIX versions from AT&T. These features included record and file locking, shared memory, semaphores, nowait input/output, and automatic file system recovery. By choosing XENIX, hardware manufacturers could avoid the work of correcting these deficiencies in their own UNIX versions.

- *Financial leverage.* Royalty payments to AT&T declined dramatically with volume. Microsoft could price XENIX attractively because the volumes from all its XENIX licensees combined to earn larger discounts under a single AT&T contract.

- *Quality control.* UNIX was developed in a research environment at Bell Labs and had a history of poor documentation, no support, and capricious changes from release to release. XENIX, however, was backed by Microsoft's commitment to support it as a commercial product.

Over time, XENIX lost these advantages. The popularity of UNIX has grown, and a number of software companies specializing in UNIX porting have sprung up; thus, hardware manufacturers can more easily buy UNIX ports for their systems. Many commercial extensions that were unique to XENIX now are incorporated into UNIX System V. AT&T also announced new licensing policies for UNIX System V that significantly reduced UNIX license fees on smaller systems, where XENIX was most important. Finally, with the introduction of System V, AT&T announced that it was committed to making UNIX a commercial product, and the result was a significant improvement in AT&T documentation and support. Release-to-release compatibility of AT&T UNIX is now required by the System V Interface Document.

With its difference from AT&T UNIX becoming a liability rather than an asset, Microsoft's XENIX was moved toward System V compatibility. Further, the combination of a System V-compatible XENIX and 80386-based systems promises a major new role for XENIX as the first mass-market multiuser operating system. XENIX has two of the essential ingredients needed to play that role: it is available on low-cost systems that can be distributed through dealers, and it will have a binary standard for mass-market software distribution. However, a third essential ingredient—widespread availability of XENIX-based applications software—remains much more of a question. Ironically, Microsoft's own OS/2 operating system casts the biggest cloud over this future XENIX role.

Before the advent of OS/2, the distinction between XENIX-based systems and personal computers was clear. MS-DOS-based PCs were limited, single-user systems. MS-DOS could perform only one task at a time, its usable memory was limited to 640 kilobytes, and its file-sharing capabilities were primitive. In contrast, XENIX-based systems possessed a clear multiuser focus. They were also much more sophisticated, supporting multiple users, megabytes of memory, and powerful file-sharing and interprocess communications features.

OS/2 blurs all these distinctions, in part because its design has borrowed heavily from UNIX. It is a multitasking operating system, allowing a user to work on several different applications in parallel. OS/2 has many of the advanced features of XENIX, such as pipes, interprocess communications, and file sharing. It runs on both personal computers and network servers, allowing users to build multiuser networks of PCs attached to a local area network. In its size, complexity, and sophistication, OS/2 is a much better alternative to XENIX than MS-DOS has been. Table 2.2 summarizes the similarities and differences between OS/2 and XENIX.

Despite their similarities, OS/2 and XENIX have quite a different focus. Like MS-DOS, OS/2 remains a personal, user-centered operating system. Its advanced features support its powerful, windowed user interface and closely cooperating tasks within a single program. Applications written for OS/2 also have the user-oriented, event-driven style of Macintosh and MS-Windows applications. XENIX remains a multiuser system, with features that support multiple, noncooperating users and place much less emphasis on user interface.

Whether these differences are enough to support two important operating systems for the 80386—one single-user and one multiuser—remains to be seen. The key question is, how will applications software developers view the role of XENIX? If software developers continue to develop XENIX-based multiuser applications, XENIX will remain an important part of the UNIX phenomenon. If they instead focus energy on networked OS/2 applications, XENIX and the 80386 will play a minor role in the evolution of UNIX.

Table 2.2
Comparison of XENIX and OS/2

	XENIX	*OS/2*
Market Position	Entry-level Multiuser System	Next Generation PC Operating System
User Focus	Multiuser	Single-user
Parallel Processing Support	Multiprogramming	Multitasking
Primary Development Language	C	C
Programming Style	Conventional	Event-driven
Key Features	Hierarchical File System Interprocess Communications File Sharing UNIX Compatibility UNIX Tools	Hierarchical File System Interprocess Communications File Sharing Windowed User Interface MS-DOS Compatibility Box

3

A Structural Overview

U NIX is a large and complex operating system. The standard UNIX system provides the user with over two hundred different commands for interacting with the system and literally thousands of options to these commands. A few of the commands are used each time a user enters the system. Others are regularly used for specialized functions, such as text processing, communications, or software development. Still other functions, such as accounting and error-checking utilities, are of interest only to system administrators. This chapter describes the overall structure of the UNIX system and provides a brief overview of each major component. The individual components are discussed in greater detail in the following chapters.

A Typical UNIX-Based System

A typical UNIX-based computer system includes a number of hardware and software components. Figure 3.1 shows a multiuser computer system, representative of those supporting UNIX. The system includes the following hardware components.

- A *system unit*, which houses the system's central processing unit and one or more disk drives for mass storage. The system unit also includes a backup device, such as a floppy disk or magnetic tape drive.

- A *console*, from which system operation is controlled. The system displays error messages on the console. It is often used as an ordinary user terminal as well.

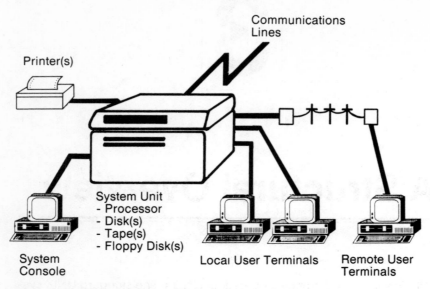

Fig. 3.1. *A Typical Multiuser UNIX-Based System*

- *User terminals*, at which users interact with the system, typing commands on the keyboard and receiving output on the display. UNIX supports user terminals that are directly attached to the computer system, as well as those that are connected to the system by communications lines and modems.

- *Communications lines*, connecting the system to other UNIX-based systems or mainframe computers.

- *Printers*, used to obtain hard-copy output. UNIX supports draft-quality printers, letter-quality printers, and even phototypesetters.

The Structure of UNIX

Figure 3.2 shows the major software components that comprise the UNIX system and their interrelationships. The major components are the following:

- The *kernel* is the core of the UNIX system, controlling the system hardware and performing various low-level functions. The other parts of the UNIX system, as well as user programs, call on the kernel to perform services for them.

- The *shell* is the command interpreter for the UNIX system. The shell accepts user commands and is responsible for seeing that they are carried out.

- Over two hundred *utility programs* are supplied with the UNIX system. These utilities (or commands) support a variety of tasks, such as copying files, editing text, performing calculations, and developing software.

- *User programs* can be developed, using the UNIX utilities, or purchased "off the shelf" from software suppliers. These programs occupy the same logical position within the UNIX system structure as that of the UNIX utilities. In fact, once installed on a UNIX system, user programs and UNIX commands are indistinguishable.

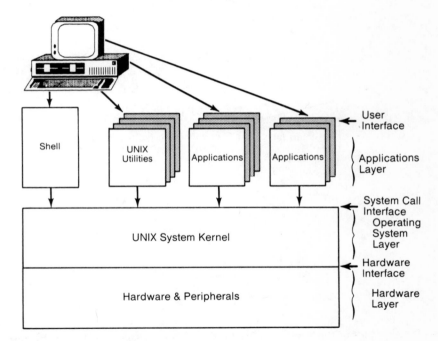

Fig. 3.2. *The Structure of UNIX*

The UNIX Kernel

The core of the UNIX system is the kernel, which performs the low-level functions that create the "UNIX environment" on a particular computer system. The kernel interacts directly with the system hardware and insulates the other parts of the UNIX system from hardware dependencies. UNIX utilities and user programs call on the kernel to perform services for them.

The functions performed by the kernel and the services it provides are shown in Figure 3.3. The kernel implements the UNIX file system, organizing and managing the system's mass storage; enforces the UNIX security scheme, which prevents unauthorized access to stored information; and performs input and output on request, transferring data to and from I/O devices.

The kernel also polices multiuser operation of the UNIX system, scheduling the central processor and ensuring that work is performed for each user who shares the system. The kernel manages the system's main memory, allocating it among the user tasks.

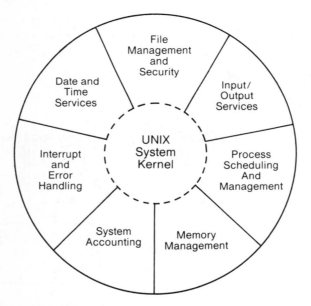

Fig. 3.3. *Function of the UNIX Kernel*

Finally, this component maintains accounting logs, recording both system activity and usage.

At the lowest level, the kernel communicates directly with the hardware. Parts of the kernel, therefore, must be custom-tailored to each particular computer system's hardware features. For example, each system manages its main memory somewhat differently, and the memory management software in the kernel must be changed to accommodate these differences. Each system also includes I/O devices with slightly different hardware characteristics. The parts of the kernel that deal directly with I/O devices, called *drivers*, must also be adapted to each new system. *Porting* a UNIX system is the process of adapting the hardware-dependent pieces of the kernel.

The UNIX System Call Interface

UNIX utilities and applications programs call on the kernel to perform services for them. The mechanism used to request kernel services is called a *system call*. Each system call instructs the kernel to perform one particular service on behalf of the program making the call. For example, each time an application program wants to read a line of user input from a terminal, the program calls the kernel, which obtains the requested data and passes it on to the program. System calls are the interface between UNIX-based applications programs and the UNIX kernel; these calls are the only way that applications programs and the kernel interact directly in a UNIX-based system. Figure 3.4 illustrates the operation of a UNIX system call.

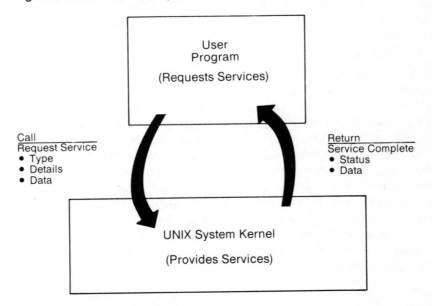

Fig. 3.4. *Anatomy of a System Call*

The UNIX kernel supports over eighty different system calls. *These calls are uniform across all UNIX-based systems.* No matter what hardware differences exist "down below," or whether the system is an IBM PC or a mainframe, the system calls are the same. Thus, the system calls form a standard interface for the UNIX system. Applications programs using only the standard system calls operate in the same way on every UNIX-based system, without modification to the programs. The commonality of the system call interface gives UNIX its vendor-independence.

The power and flexibility of the UNIX system calls make the kernel a powerful base for executing user-developed and off-the-shelf applications programs. In a real sense, the kernel's system call interface *is* the UNIX system. Most of the work on UNIX standards during the past five years has focused on developing a formal standard for the system call interface.

The standardization of UNIX at the system call interface is in marked contrast to the standardization of MS-DOS on the IBM PC. To be sure, MS-DOS also has a standard system call interface, but software developers have found it inadequate for their needs. As a result, popular PC software programs "reach around" the MS-DOS system calls to interact directly with the PC's Basic Input/Output System (BIOS) and the PC hardware in order to perform such tasks as screen display, keyboard input, and communications. The MS-DOS standard includes not only MS-DOS but also the specifics of the BIOS and the hardware features of the IBM PC. More than one PC manufacturer has discovered this factor the hard way—through market rejection of a personal computer that offered MS-DOS but was incompatible with the IBM PC BIOS and hardware.

The difference between the standardizations of UNIX and MS-DOS has important implications for the two systems. For example, the difference defines the parts of the computer market where each operating system can have an impact. MS-DOS dominates the personal computer market but also is confined to that market segment. Even if a version of MS-DOS were developed for minicomputers, that version's influence would be minimal because the popular MS-DOS software applications, which depend on the PC hardware, could not run on the minicomputers. In contrast, UNIX is available on a broad range of systems, from PCs to mainframes. Because the UNIX standard insulates applications programs from hardware dependencies, the same applications can easily be moved to any UNIX-based system. Therefore, UNIX system call standardization allows UNIX to play an important role on a much broader variety of computer systems.

The low-level standard for MS-DOS has one critical advantage that the UNIX standard lacks, however: software portability at the object code level. Because all MS-DOS-based systems have Intel processors and PC-compatible hardware, a compiled program runs on all IBM PC-compatibles without recompilation. This binary compatibility allows mass-market distribution of PC software through computer stores, mail order firms, and bookstores. A copy of 1-2-3®, for example, purchased for an IBM

PC, also runs on many other "PC clones" because of this object code portability.

In contrast, the UNIX standard provides only *source code* compatibility among UNIX systems. Various UNIX-based systems are implemented using different processors, different input/output systems, and different hardware designs. Real world UNIX-based systems exhibit this broad diversity, ranging from PCs (with Intel microprocessors) to engineering workstations (often Motorola processors) to super-minicomputers (with a wide range of proprietary processors).

The source code for a UNIX application can be moved to each of these UNIX systems, compiled into object code form, and executed. When executed on the various systems, the compiled form of the program produces the same behavior on each system. However, the actual object code of the program is *different* on each system. Users cannot move the object code from one system to another; the actual instructions and data formats of the systems are incompatible.

The difference between the object code standard for MS-DOS applications and the source code standard for UNIX applications has had a major impact on the market for the two operating systems. The explosion of MS-DOS usage on PCs is largely due to the development of a mass market for MS-DOS applications, with the associated distribution channels and relatively low prices. A single copy of an MS-DOS application on a computer retailer's shelf works with *every* PC-compatible system in the store.

In contrast, a copy of a UNIX application for an NCR system, for example, works only on NCR systems. A Sun workstation requires a different copy, and a Tandy XENIX system requires still a different copy. Although all the copies are derived from the same source code, the UNIX software developer must create, distribute, and support a different object copy of an application on each supported UNIX system. Thus, one key advantage of UNIX—its portability across widely different systems—also prevents the development of a mass market for UNIX software and retards the growth of UNIX applications.

The Shell

In the UNIX system, the shell is the component that interacts directly with the user. The shell is a command interpreter. It accepts commands from the user and causes them to be carried out, one by one. In addition, a number of convenience features provided by the shell make command entry easier and give the user more flexibility in controlling UNIX operation. Chapter 5 describes the shell in detail.

The UNIX Utilities

The UNIX utilities are a collection of more than three hundred programs that are supplied with the UNIX system for performing particular functions. These utilities are the UNIX *commands*, which are invoked, by name, through the shell. As previously explained, the kernel by itself offers only a set of low-level services for performing simple functions. The utilities organize these services into a set of useful user-level functions.

The UNIX utilities cover a wide range of functions, from editing, copying, and erasing files to sending and receiving electronic mail messages to managing the progress of a large software-development project. A core of about two dozen utilities are familiar to most UNIX users as part of their everyday command repertoire. Most users also use some of the more advanced utilities in particular areas that apply to their jobs, such as the text-processing or software-development utilities. Virtually no UNIX user is familiar with the entire set of utilities.

In the latest release of UNIX System V, AT&T divided the utilities into functional groups, making them easier to install and manage on a UNIX system. Some of the more interesting groups follow:

- *Essential utilities* are used daily by almost all UNIX users.

- *Directory- and file-management utilities* are used for managing the UNIX file and directory structure.

- *Editing utilities* are used for editing documents, programs, and other text files.

- *Spell utilities* detect spelling errors in text files.

- *Help utilities* provide on-line help with UNIX commands.

- *Line printer spooling utilities* allow users to share access to a line printer and let the system manager control the printer's operation.

- *Graphics utilities* analyze data and transform it into graphs and charts on graphics terminals and other output devices.

- *Basic networking utilities* allow UNIX users to send and receive files from other UNIX systems and to execute remote UNIX commands.

- *Networking support utilities* provide a standardized interface to various communications links and support development of new communications products.

- *Remote file-sharing utilities* give UNIX users direct access to shared files and other resources on remote UNIX systems.

- *C Programming utilities* support development of applications programs in the C programming language.

- *Advanced programming utilities* support advanced C program development and help coordinate the work of programmers in large software-development projects.

- *Terminal information utilities* describe the many different kinds of terminals that can be connected to a UNIX system and help programmers develop terminal-independent applications.

- *Interprocess communications utilities* manage the communications between programs on a UNIX system.

- *Security administration utilities* let a user encrypt data stored in UNIX files.

- *System administration utilities* help a system manager keep the system running smoothly and support administrative tasks like authorizing new users and backing up the system.

- *Performance measurement utilities* help a system manager fine-tune the performance of a UNIX system.

The most commonly used UNIX utilities in these utility groups are described in Chapters 4 through 11.

Unfortunately, as utilities have been developed and added to the UNIX system over the years, the utilities have been given short names that only vaguely describe their functions. For example, the UNIX command to display the names of the files in the current directory is an abbreviated form of the word *list*, **ls**. Consequently, the commands are easy to type but difficult to remember and understand. For this reason, UNIX is sometimes criticized as an "unfriendly" system.

UNIX Applications

In addition to the utilities that are provided as part of the UNIX operating system, more than a thousand UNIX-based applications programs are available from independent software developers. The availability of these off-the-shelf applications is one of the major attractions of the UNIX system. The following list illustrates just some of the categories of applications software available for UNIX-based systems:

- *Database management.* Relational database management systems have had a remarkable penetration into the UNIX systems market. More than a dozen different database management systems are available, and many have associated fourth-generation languages that speed the development of forms-based interactive applications.

- *Word processing.* UNIX systems are widely used for word processing and other office automation applications. Available word processors include WANG-compatible products, packages common to UNIX and MS-DOS systems, and products developed specifically to support technical writing.

- *Accounting.* A number of standard accounting packages have been ported to UNIX-based systems. Some of these packages have been moved from other proprietary minicomputer operating systems; others are upgraded versions of PC accounting packages.

- *Language processors.* UNIX began as a vehicle for software development, so the proliferation of compilers for Ada, BASIC, C, COBOL, DIBOL, FORTRAN, Lisp, Pascal, Prolog, PL/I, RPG, and many other languages is not surprising. Many artificial-intelligence applications-development tools also run under UNIX.

- *Computer-aided engineering.* The dominance of UNIX on engineering workstations has created a rich set of applications for circuit design and simulation, structural analysis, mechanical design, fluid dynamics, and other engineering support functions.

- *Communications.* Communications utilities are available to link UNIX systems to personal computers, to non-UNIX minicomputers, and to mainframe systems, using popular industry standard protocols such as TCP/IP, XNS, X.25, and SNA.

Although the list of UNIX applications packages grows every day, it remains dwarfed by the collection of software available for PCs under MS-DOS. In addition, the absence of an object code standard for UNIX software complicates the availability of UNIX applications.

To purchase a UNIX application program, the buyer must first locate a source for the program; this source may be the UNIX system manufacturer, the software developer, or a software distributor (but probably will *not* be the corner computer store). The buyer must also insure that the application performs the required functions *and* that it is available in a version for his or her particular UNIX system. Despite these difficulties, the market for UNIX applications software is thriving, and many popular packages have tens of thousands of installations.

The File System

One of the most powerful and attractive features of UNIX is the file system, which manages data stored on the computer's mass storage devices. The file system's facilities make it easy to organize stored information in a very natural way and to retrieve and modify it, as necessary. Many of the file system's features were unique when UNIX was first created, and they have been so popular that they have since been duplicated in other commercial operating systems. This chapter provides a detailed discussion of the file system's capabilities.

File System Features and Benefits

The UNIX file system includes the following major features:

- *Hierarchical structure.* Users can group together related information and efficiently manipulate a group of files as a unit. The resulting organization resembles the operation of manual filing systems.

- *File expansion.* Files grow dynamically, as needed, taking up only the amount of mass storage space required to store their current contents. The user is not forced to decide in advance how large a file will grow.

- *Structureless files.* UNIX imposes no internal structure on a file's contents. The user is free to structure and interpret the contents of a file in whatever way is appropriate.

- *Security.* Files can be protected against unauthorized use by different users of the UNIX system.

- *File and device independence.* UNIX treats files and input/output devices identically. The same procedures and programs used to process information stored in files can be used to read data from a terminal, print it on a printer, or pass it to another program.

- *File sharing.* Several application programs can access a file concurrently to read or update its contents. UNIX provides methods to coordinate file access and maintain data integrity.

The Concept of a File

The fundamental structure that UNIX uses to store information is the *file*. UNIX files have much in common with the file folders used every day in business. Like file folders, UNIX files store diverse kinds of information. A file can store payroll data, word-processing documents, programming instructions that tell the system how to execute daily procedures, and even excerpts from the UNIX documentation. In short, UNIX files are the structure used to store virtually every kind of information required for the operation of a typical UNIX system.

UNIX keeps track of files internally by assigning each one a unique identifying number. Thus, a customer file may be stored in file number 2217, inventory transactions may be stored in file number 456, and so on. On a typical multiuser UNIX system, it is not unusual to have thousands of files existing at any one time.

Obviously, identifying files by number can be very tedious; and in practice, file numbers, called *inode numbers*, are used only within the UNIX system itself. Instead of requiring file numbers of users, the file system allows them to identify each file by a user-assigned name. A *file name* can be any sequence containing from one to fourteen characters—usually more than enough to describe meaningfully the file's contents. But even this method poses a problem for a multiuser system with thousands of files. For example, how can a user be certain, when assigning a name to a new file, that the name selected has not been used previously by some other user?

The Concept of a Directory

UNIX provides users a way of organizing files by grouping them into direc-tories. A *directory* performs the same function as a file drawer in a filing cabi-net, gathering together related files in a common place where they can be found easily.

With directories, the user has complete flexibility in grouping files in a mean-ingful way. For example, a business might maintain files of information on sales results, customer orders, forecasts, and personnel—for each of its sales offices. A sensible way to organize this information is to create a di-rectory for each sales office, with each directory containing only those files that relate to that particular office.

UNIX directories themselves have names, each of which may also contain up to fourteen characters. Again, names describing the kinds of files in the directory are usually chosen. For example, the files for the Boston sales of-fice might be called **results**, **orders**, **forecast**, and **personnel**. The directory containing these files might then be called **boston**. Another common use of directories is to give one to each user, with the directory's name being that of the user. The user's files are then identified through the user's own direc-tory, eliminating any confusion with the files of others.

Internally, a directory is just a special file, which contains a list of file names and their corresponding inode numbers. The directory performs exactly the same function as a common telephone directory. Given the name of a file, UNIX looks in the directory and obtains the corresponding inode number for the file. With this number, the file system can examine other internal tables to determine where the file is stored and to make it accessible to the user. Figure 4.1 shows how directories are used to locate files.

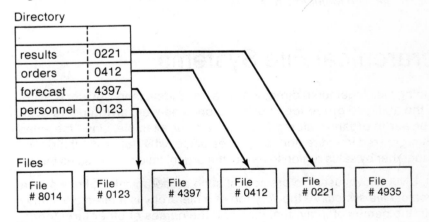

Fig. 4.1. *A UNIX Directory*

Files with Several Names

A file name is merely a means to identify a file to the UNIX system. In fact, one file may be identified by two or more names! A single file may also be identified in more than one directory. UNIX calls this "having multiple links to a file," since there is more than one way for a user to identify the file. Multiple links can be useful when more than one user needs access to a file. For example, a sales report may be of interest to several different managers in a company. Without duplicating the file's contents, each manager may call the file by the manager's own name and identify the file through that manager's private directory. Figure 4.2 shows such an arrangement.

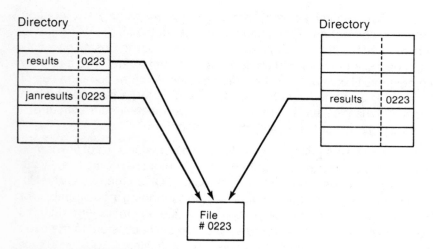

Fig. 4.2. *A File with Multiple Links*

Hierarchical File Systems

If grouping files together in directories is a good idea, then why not provide users the ability to group together directories as well, giving users even more power to organize stored information? For example, since the sales data is organized into directories by sales office, why not group the directories together by sales region to reflect the organization of the sales force?

In fact, UNIX allows users to create just such an organization, known as a *hierarchical file system*. At the very top of a hierarchy is a directory. It may contain the names of individual files and the names of other directories.

These, in turn, may contain the names of individual files and the names of still other directories, and so on. A hierarchy of files is the result.

The UNIX file hierarchy resembles an upside-down tree, with its root at the top. The various directories branch out until they finally trace a path to the individual files, which correspond to the tree's leaves. You will often hear the UNIX file system described as "tree-structures," with the single directory at the very top of the hierarchy called the *root directory*. The name of the root directory is */*. All the files that can be reached by tracing a path down through the directory hierarchy from the root directory are called a *file system*.

Figure 4.3 shows a file system that might be used for a sales organization. Files for each sales office are grouped into a directory for that office, and these directories are, in turn, grouped by sales region. An additional directory stores programs used to process the data in the sales office files. All the directories relating to the application are grouped under the single directory **sales**.

Path Names

A typical UNIX file system will have many levels in its hierarchy; ten levels from top to bottom are not uncommon. Each file in the file system may be uniquely identified by giving its path name. A *path name* is nothing more than a list of the directories, by name, that lie along the path from the root to the individual file, followed by the file's own name. By convention, the names in a path name are separated by slashes, and the path name begins with a slash to indicate that the name starts at the root directory**. Thus the name

/sales/east/boston/forecast

is the path name for one of the files in Figure 4.3. Path names that trace a complete path down from the root directory are called *fully qualified* path names because they describe the complete path that UNIX must take to locate the file.

Partial Path Names

Identifying each file by its full path name can be very cumbersome. In practice, most users work with only a small set of files at one time. Often these files will be grouped together in a single directory. UNIX allows the user to designate this directory as the user's *current working directory*.

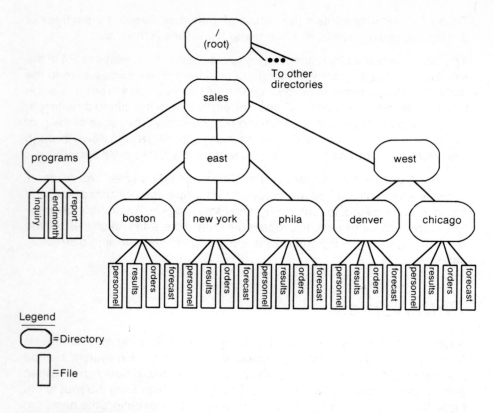

Fig. 4.3. *A UNIX File System*

As a convenience, users can use a shorthand notation, known as a *partially qualified* path name, to identify a file whose path name includes the current working directory. This path name simply omits the initial slash and the directory names up to and including the current working directory. In Figure 4.3, if the current working directory is **/sales/east**, then the partially qualified path name of

boston/forecast

identifies the same file as the one identified with a fully qualified path name in the earlier example.

Two special UNIX notations make partial path names even more powerful for navigating through the directory hierarchy. A single dot (**.**) is used to indicate the current working directory. It is used frequently in commands that can take a directory name as an argument. For example, the UNIX copy command can be used to copy a file into a particular destination directory, which is specified as the copy command's last argument. Suppose that a user wants to copy a file into the current working directory; the user can specify the argument with a single dot rather than spell out the directory name.

A double dot (**..**) is used to indicate *upward* motion through the directory hierarchy to the parent of a directory. For example, if the current working directory in Figure 4.3 is **/sales/east**, then the partial path name

   ../west/denver

specifies the **/sales/west/denver** directory. The partial path name tells the UNIX system to start at the current working directory, move up one level (..), move down to the **west** directory, and finally move down to the **denver** directory. The double-dot syntax can be used repeatedly to move up several levels in the hierarchy. For example, if **/sales/east** is the current working directory, then the partial path

   ../..

specifies the root directory.

File Information

UNIX maintains a great deal of information about the files that it manages. For each file, the file system keeps track of the following:

- Location — Where is the file stored on the disk?
- Size — How large is the file?
- Link count — By how many names is the file known?
- Ownership — Which user "owns" the file?
- Security — Which users may access the file?
- Type — Is the file a directory or not?
- Creation — When was the file created?
- Modification — When was the file last modified?
- Access — When was the file last accessed?

All of this information is maintained automatically by the file system as the files are created and used. The information is used by several utilities to process files selectively. For example, the UNIX backup utilities can save copies of only those files that were modified since some specified past date. The time of the last modification is used to select the appropriate files.

Multiple Disks

Most UNIX-based computer systems have at least one permanent, nonremovable hard disk as their principal mass storage. The files stored on this disk are always accessible by the system. The root directory and the file system below it are stored on this disk. This file system is called the *root file system*.

Most UNIX-based computers also support additional hard disks, allowing expansion of the system's mass storage capacity. UNIX manages the files on these disks by creating a separate file system on each hard disk. In other words, each disk has its own complete hierarchical file system, with its own root. The file system on each disk is independent of those on other disks.

Before the file system on an additional hard disk can be used, the file system must be made accessible to UNIX. This is done by attaching the file system to the root file system, making the attached file system part of the root directory hierarchy. Figure 4.4 illustrates this process of *mounting* a file system. Once the file system has been mounted, its files are accessible as if they were a permanent part of the root file system. Path names for files on the mounted file system begin at the root of the root file system and then branch down through the mounted file system to locate the file.

The process of mounting a file system can be reversed by *unmounting* it, that is, severing its connection to the root. Mounting and unmounting file systems are accomplished through UNIX utility commands. Generally, file systems are mounted as part of the UNIX system start-up sequence and are not unmounted until the system shuts down; users, therefore, perceive these file systems as a permanent part of the file hierarchy.

UNIX also allows a single hard disk to be divided into several independent file systems, which can be separately mounted and unmounted. This technique is useful in tuning the performance of a UNIX system or sheltering private data from unauthorized access.

Mountable file systems are also used to organize files on floppy disks. When a floppy disk is inserted into a disk drive, the user must first mount the floppy's file system before using the files in it. Similarly, before the floppy disk is removed from the drive, its file system must be unmounted.

Input/Output Devices

Printers, terminals, tape drives, and many other types of input and output devices can all be connected to a UNIX system. The file system extends the concept of a file to include all these devices. They are treated as *special files*, which are accessed as if they were simply ordinary files on the system. By convention, all the I/O devices on a UNIX system are given individual file names and grouped together in a directory named **/dev** (short for "devices"). By tradition, standard names are assigned to the most common devices, as listed in Table 4.1. Most UNIX utilities and off-the-shelf applications programs assume that the devices have these names.

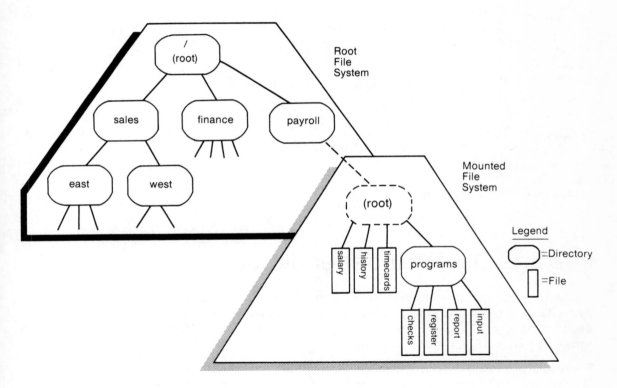

Fig. 4.4. *A Mounted File System*

Table 4.1
Typical UNIX System Device Names

/dev/lp	{	System printer
/dev/dk0 /dev/dk1 ⋮	}	disks
/dev/rdk0 /dev/rdk1 ⋮	}	disks, as "raw" I/O devices
/dev/mt0 /dev/mt1 ⋮	}	magnetic tape drives
/dev/rmt0 /dev/rmt1 ⋮	}	magnetic tape drives, as "raw" I/O devices
/dev/tty0 /dev/tty1 /dev/tty2 ⋮	}	terminals or communications lines
/dev/null	{	a "null" file

File and Device Independence

Input and output operations to I/O devices work exactly the same as for ordinary files. Applications programs designed to work with files can thus work with all types of I/O devices, with no changes needed. This feature is known as *file and device independence*.

The benefit of treating I/O devices as ordinary files can be simply illustrated. The following UNIX command is used to copy a file named **orders** to a file named **results**:

   cp orders results

The same command can be used to "copy" the file to the printer:

   cp orders /dev/lp

File and device independence allows a single utility program to be used for many different functions. On operating systems that do not provide this feature, each of these functions must be handled by a separate utility program, adding to the complexity of the system and making the functions more difficult to learn. Figure 4.5 illustrates the file and device independence provided by the UNIX file system.

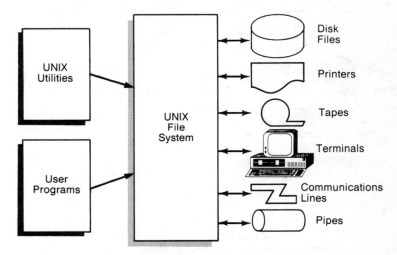

Fig. 4.5. *File and Device Independence*

The Standard File Hierarchy

UNIX uses its hierarchical file system to organize its own system files. Individual directories are used to store the various components of the UNIX system. For example, the directory **/bin** (short for "binary" object files) stores the UNIX utilities. The **/etc** directory stores miscellaneous administrative utilities and information, such as the file listing authorized users of the system. The **/tmp** directory stores temporary files. The kernel itself is stored in the file named **/unix**. Table 4.2 lists the directories typically used to store the component parts of the UNIX system.

In many UNIX systems, each user is given a directory, where all of the user's private files and directories are stored. These user directories are often set up as subdirectories of a directory named **/usr**. Thus, Sam's files will appear in the directory **/usr/sam**, and Mary's files, in the directory **/usr/mary**. Figure 4.6 shows these user directories and their relationship to the system directories listed in Table 4.2.

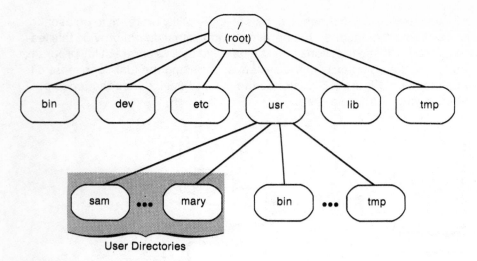

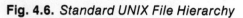

User Directories

Fig. 4.6. *Standard UNIX File Hierarchy*

Table 4.2
Directories Used by the UNIX System

/bin	UNIX utilities
/dev	Special files (I/O devices)
/etc	Administrative programs and tables
/lib	Libraries used by the UNIX language processors
/tmp	Temporary files
/usr/bin	UNIX utilities (overflow for **/bin**)
/usr/adm	Administrative commands and files
/usr/games	Game programs
/usr/include	Include files used by the UNIX language processors
/usr/lib	Archive libraries, text-processing macros
/usr/mail	Mail files
/usr/news	News files
/usr/spool	Spool files for printing
/usr/src	Program source files
/usr/tmp	Temporary files

File Management Utilities

Several UNIX utilities are tools for managing files and the information they contain. There are utilities for creating new files and directories, for removing unused files from the system, for copying files, and so on. Table 4.3 lists the most frequently used file management utilities.

Table 4.3
File Management Utilities

pwd	Prints the name of the current working directory
cd	Changes the current working directory
ls	Lists the contents of directories
cat	Concatenates files
mv	Moves and renames files
ln	Creates a new link (name) for a file
cp	Copies files
mkdir	Creates new directories
rm	Removes files
rmdir	Removes directories
du	Displays disk usage
df	Displays the number of free blocks for mounted file systems
touch	Updates the time of last modification for files
find	Locates files that match certain criteria

The command descriptions that follow include examples of typical command use. For each example, the user's current working directory is **sales/east/boston**, and the file system shown in Figure 4.3 applies.

Identifying the Current Working Directory

The **pwd** (**p**rint **w**orking **d**irectory) utility displays the fully qualified path name of the current working directory:

```
$ pwd
/sales/east/boston
$ ■
```

The **pwd** utility is one of the simplest of UNIX utilities. It has no options, takes no input, and produces a single line of output.

Moving to a Different Current Working Directory

The **cd** (**c**hange **w**orking **d**irectory) utility moves the user into a different working directory. For example, if files for the New York sales office are to be used heavily for the next few commands, the command

```
$ cd /sales/east/newyork
$ ■
```

makes **newyork** the current working directory. The New York files can now be conveniently accessed with partially qualified path names.

Listing the File Names in a Directory

The **ls** (**l**ist) utility lists the files in a directory. For example, to list the files in **/sales/east/phila**, type this command:

```
$ ls /sales/east/phila
forecast
orders
personnel
results
$ ■
```

Omitting the directory name in the command gives a listing of the files in the current working directory. The **ls** command has many options that are used to display different information about the files, such as the date and time of last access and modification, whether the file is an ordinary file or a directory, etc. One of the most often used options is the so-called "long" option, which produces a very detailed output, illustrated in Figure 4.7.

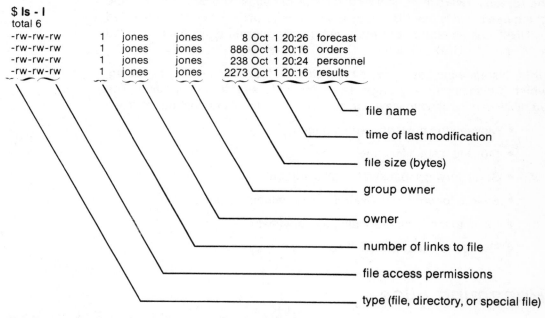

Fig. 4.7. *File Information from the LS Command*

Viewing File Contents

The **cat** (con**cat**enate files) command is often used to view the contents of a file on a terminal screen. As the name suggests, **cat** is a general-purpose utility, which is more fully described in Chapter 8. Displaying file contents, however, is probably this utility's most frequent use. The file names specified in the command are displayed in sequence on the screen, as in the following example:

```
$ cat personnel
John R. Jones      Dist. Mgr. 1200000    1036000     86%
Paul N. Davis      Salesman   1000000     856730     83%
Mike E. Smith      Salesman    900000    1034360    115%
James R. Harris    Salesman    850000     674390     79%
Dan A. Andrews     Salesman    800000     850340    106%
$ ▪
```

Note that the **cat** utility displays the entire file, line by line, without pause. An alternative utility, called **more**, is offered as part of the Berkeley UNIX system. This utility pauses after displaying a screenful of data, allowing page-by-page browsing through a file. Single-character commands to **more** move the screen forward through the file by lines or pages. The **more** utility is one of the most widely used Berkeley extensions to UNIX. It is often supported by UNIX system manufacturers, even if their operating system is derived from an AT&T UNIX version.

UNIX System V includes a more sophisticated file-viewing utility called **pg**, which provides page-by-page viewing and file-searching capability. The **pg** utility can be used to view one or more files and offers commands to

- Move to the next/preceding page
- Move to a specific page
- Scroll forward/backward half a screen
- Search forward/backward for text matching a pattern
- Move to the next/preceding file for viewing
- Escape to execute a shell command

Renaming Files

The **mv** (**move**) utility changes the name of a file. Both the old and new names for the file are given with this command:

```
$ mv forecast prediction
$ ■
```

In this example, the name of a file is changed from **forecast** to **prediction**. The **mv** utility can rename directories in the same way. The command

```
$ mv /sales/east /sales/northeast
$ ■
```

is used to rename the eastern sales region's directory if the name of the sales territory is changed.

Some kinds of "renaming" of a file actually result in a file having a different position in the file system hierarchy. For example, the command

```
$ mv forecast /sales/east/newyork/forecast
$ ■
```

"moves" the **forecast** file from the **boston** directory to the **newyork** directory. In effect, renaming the file has moved it to a new directory. The name of the command suggests this possible use.

Linking File Names

Recall that a file may be known in the UNIX system by several different names. The **ln** (**link**) command is used to give a file additional names. Both the current name and the new name are given with the following command:

```
$ ln /sales/east/newyork/forecast  fantasy
$ ■
```

The New York **forecast** file is now also identified as **fantasy**. There is still only one copy of the file.

Copying Files

The **cp** (**cop**y) utility makes a duplicate copy of a file. For example, the command

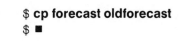

```
$ cp forecast oldforecast
$ ■
```

duplicates the contents of the **forecast** file and calls it **oldforecast**. Two separate files result, and changes to one of the files do not affect the other copy of the data.

Making New Directories

The **mkdir** (**make dir**ectory) utility creates a new directory. For example, the command

```
$ mkdir /sales/east/atlanta
$ ■
```

might be used to make a directory for a new sales office in Atlanta. The newly created directory is *empty*; that is, it contains no files.

Removing File Names

The **rm** (**rem**ove) command removes unwanted file names from the directory, as in the following:

```
$ rm fantasy
$ ■
```

If the file to be removed is known by more than one name, only the specified name for the file is removed; the other names and the data itself remain. (In this example, the name **fantasy** is removed.) The contents of a file are actually erased from the system only when the last name identifying the file is removed.

To prevent a major accident, the **rm** utility will not ordinarily remove directories. However, an option is available that will delete a directory, as well as all the files and subdirectories that it contains. Thus, the command

```
$ rm -r /sales/west
$ ■
```

removes all the files and directories for the western sales region, including the directory **west** itself.

Removing Directories

The **rmdir** (**rem**ove **dir**ectory) utility removes directories that are no longer needed. The name of the directory to be removed is given in the following command:

```
$ rm dir /sales/east/atlanta
$ ■
```

As a safeguard, the **rmdir** utility will only remove directories that are empty.

Internal File Structure*

Unlike most operating systems, UNIX does not impose a rigid internal structure on the contents of files. In fact, UNIX cares very little about the internal organization of files and provides only one file organization. All UNIX files are treated as a simple sequence of bytes (characters), beginning with the first byte in the file and ending with the last one. An individual byte within the file is identified by its position, relative to the beginning of the file, as shown in Figure 4.8.

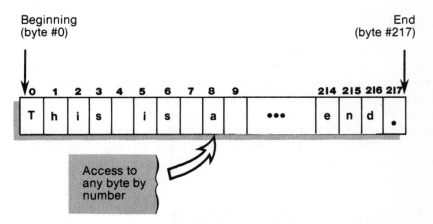

Fig. 4.8. *Internal UNIX File Organization*

Most other microcomputer operating systems force users to organize files into *records* or *blocks* of one fixed length. This requirement corresponds to the way that data is organized on the disk. These structures frequently hamper, rather than enhance, the development of applications software. CP/M, for example, uses blocks of 128 bytes. But a report file may naturally be organized as a sequence of 80-character lines, a customer file may contain two-thousand character records for each customer, and a document may contain a sequence of paragraphs that vary in length. Programs accessing these files must translate their requirements for accessing lines, records, and paragraphs into requests for one or more blocks from the disk. This method prevents programs from organizing the data in the most natural way for the application.

UNIX specifically shields the user from the concept of records or blocks. Instead, UNIX can deliver, on request, a particular byte or sequence of bytes from anywhere in the file. Programs are thus free to organize their files independent of the way the data is actually stored on the disk. The simple internal structure of UNIX files makes access to their contents very simple, too. Information needed from a file is identified by giving its starting position in the file and the length of the data needed. Similarly, information can be placed into a file in any position, again by giving the starting position in the file where the data is to be placed and its length.

Although the "structureless" files of UNIX offer flexibility, disadvantages do exist. In fact, most data-processing files do have a record-oriented structure. And with UNIX, knowledge of that structure must be contained within the application programs that process the file. For example, all the programs that work with a payroll master file must understand its record structure. Even a simple change in the record structure, such as adding a new data item, requires a change in each program that uses the file, complicating software maintenance.

During the last few years, a major trend in commercial data-processing software has been to reduce this dependency of application programs on the specific structure of a file. For example, relational database management systems insulate the applications that process a database from the structure and format of the data itself. In fact, relational database packages are among the most popular of UNIX applications, precisely because they both impose a record structure on UNIX files and insulate application programs from that structure.

Disk Storage Allocation*

The UNIX file system uses advanced techniques for managing disk storage. As information is added to files, UNIX allows them to grow dynamically. The maximum size of a UNIX file is quite large—in excess of two billion bytes.

However, unlike operating systems that force users to reserve space in advance for the maximum size a file may achieve, UNIX files take up only as much space as they actually need. When a file is deleted, its disk space is made available to store other files.

UNIX organizes a disk as a sequence of 1,024-byte *blocks*. The contents of a file are stored in one or more blocks, which may be widely scattered on the disk. A list of the locations of the first ten blocks of a file is stored in the file's *inode*, along with other critical information. The inode is generally available in main memory; therefore, data in the first ten blocks of a file requires only one disk access for retrieval. UNIX thus maximizes the efficiency of processing short files, somewhat at the expense of processing long ones.

If a file is longer than ten blocks, UNIX begins to use "indirect access" techniques. The locations of subsequent blocks of the file are stored, not in the inode, but in another disk block, called an *indirect block*. The location of the indirect block is stored in the inode. Thus, access to data in the eleventh block of a file requires two disk accesses—one to retrieve the indirect block and one to retrieve the actual data block. This *single-indirect* access suffices for most commonly encountered files. Figure 4.9 shows how indirect file access works.

Of course, the indirect block itself can hold only a limited number of block locations, and eventually its capacity is also exhausted. UNIX handles files beyond this limit with a *double-indirect* method. Stored in the inode is the location of one double-indirect block, which contains the locations of many single-indirect blocks. The single-indirect blocks, in turn, contain the locations of blocks of the file.

Double indirection requires three disk accesses for every file access. This method suffices for large files.

UNIX permits one more level of indirection, known as *triple-indirect* access, for handling very large files (up to several billion bytes). Another layer is simply added to the scheme, with the location of a triple-indirect block stored in the inode. This block contains the location of double-indirect blocks, which contain the locations of single-indirect blocks, and so on.

The UNIX disk-storage allocation scheme described here has a significant impact on performance as a file becomes larger. Short files that can be handled without indirection are processed most efficiently. But as single, double, and triple indirection are required, more physical disk I/O is required to access a block of data in the file.

The same performance impact occurs as a UNIX directory grows larger, because a directory is just a special file that holds information about other files. When the number of directory entries expands so that indirection is required

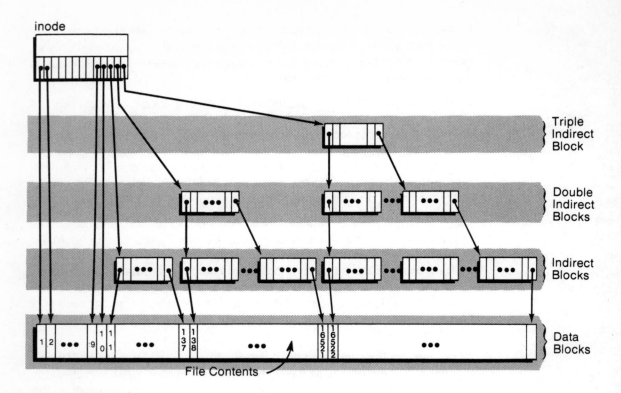

Fig. 4.9. *UNIX File Access*

to access data blocks in the directory file, the speed of directory searches slows significantly. Because directories are searched often during normal UNIX operation (e.g., to start a program or to open a file), the user usually should break larger directories into several smaller ones.

Some versions of the UNIX system incorporate modifications to the UNIX file system to improve disk performance. The Berkeley versions of the UNIX file system, for example, use a 4,096-byte block size. This larger block size results in less I/O activity and allows larger files to be handled at each level of indirection. However, the larger size also results in more wasted space because the last block of a file will be, on the average, half unused.

Disk Buffering*

On many microcomputer systems, input and output to disk files are actually performed at the time these activities are requested by an application program. That is, each request to read data from a file or to write data into a file produces actual disk I/O activity. While this technique may offer adequate performance for simple personal computer applications, the technique quickly leads to performance problems under the heavy disk I/O load of a typical multiuser UNIX system.

To minimize the amount of disk I/O actually performed, the UNIX file system uses a sophisticated technique, called *buffering*. With this technique, some of the blocks of data from the disk are duplicated in main memory by UNIX. A typical multiuser system may have as many as 64 or even 128 disk blocks duplicated in these *disk buffers*.

Figure 4.10 shows how disk buffering works. When a user program tries to read data from the disk, the file system first checks the disk buffers to see whether the required disk block is already present there. If so, the read request can be satisfied without actual disk activity. Similarly, if the program is updating data on the disk, and the corresponding disk block is in one of the disk buffers, UNIX merely modifies the data in the buffer. The contents of the disk buffer will actually be written onto the disk at a later time.

The file system automatically manages the disk buffers. When a user program requires a block of data that is not in one of the disk buffers, the file system decides which of the blocks currently in the buffers will be replaced by the new block. If the block to be replaced has been modified while in the buffer, that block must first be copied to the disk before the new block can be brought in the place of the modified block.

These techniques eliminate many disk I/O operations. Only the first request to read a disk block results in actual disk activity. The information for subsequent reads comes from the buffer. Similarly, repeated requests to write a disk block will only modify the copy of the block in the buffers. An actual disk write occurs only when a modified block of data in the disk buffers is finally replaced. Buffering improves system performance because user programs tend to access the same disk blocks over and over again. The majority of disk I/O requests, therefore, do not result in actual disk I/O.

The UNIX disk-buffering technique has one major disadvantage. If a critical system error (a "crash") occurs, the system halts, and the data in the disk buffers never is copied to the disk. When the system is restarted, some of the files on the disk may be corrupted as a result. Some modified blocks from these files are copied to the disk; others are lost in the system crash, with

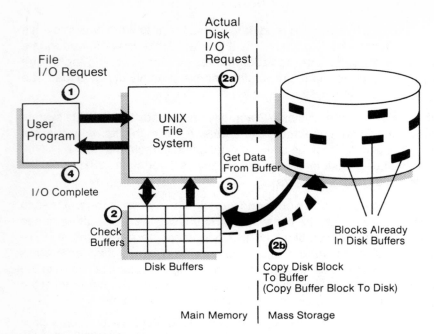

Fig. 4.10. *UNIX File System Buffering*

their *unmodified* versions still on the disk. If one of the corrupted blocks is an indirect block, the consequences can be worse: the pointers that locate the data blocks of a file also are lost. Finally, if a block of a directory file is corrupted, entire files may be lost.

Modern UNIX systems have adopted several techniques to deal with the potentially dangerous consequences of disk buffering during a system crash. One common technique is to force periodically the UNIX system to copy all its modified buffers to disk. The **sync** utility performs this function, and UNIX systems often are configured to run **sync** every 30 seconds; this procedure limits the impact of system failures to work done in the last half-minute.

Power failures are a frequent cause of system crashes, so battery backup of main memory is another commonly used technique. A power failure causes a system with battery backup to enter a dormant state, but the contents of main memory are preserved by power from a battery. When power is restored, the system can be restarted with its memory still intact, and the modified disk buffers can be written properly to the disk.

In addition to prevention techniques such as these, the UNIX system includes utilities that enable recovery from file corruption. In normal operation, UNIX maintains somewhat redundant information on a disk about the file systems it contains. The recovery utilities examine this information at a low level and use its redundancy to perform limited reconstruction of corrupted files.

The Shell

The shell is the most frequently used utility program on a standard UNIX system. UNIX places a user in conversation with the shell at the beginning of each work session with the computer. The user interacts with the shell repeatedly during the session, giving it commands that direct the work of the system on the user's behalf. When the work session is complete, the shell controls termination of the session.

The shell is a sophisticated UNIX utility program. It is the UNIX system's *command interpreter*. The role of the shell is very simple: it "prompts" the user for commands and causes the UNIX system to obey them. Interacting with the user through the keyboard and the terminal display, the shell manages the dialogue between the computer user and the UNIX system. The shell most commonly used on UNIX systems is called the Bourne shell, named after its developer. Other shells have been developed; they are described briefly at the end of this chapter.

Shell Features and Benefits

The UNIX system's shell includes the following major features:

- *Interactive processing.* Communication between the user and the UNIX system takes the form of an interactive dialogue with the shell.

- *Background processing.* Time-consuming, noninteractive tasks can proceed while the user continues with other interactive processing. The system can perform many different tasks at the same time on behalf of a single user.

- *Input/output redirection.* Programs designed to interact with a user can easily be instructed to take their input from another source, such as a file, and send their output to another destination, such as a printer.

- *Pipes.* Programs that perform simple functions can easily be connected together to perform more complex functions, minimizing the need to develop new programs.

- *Wild-card matching.* The user can specify a pattern to select one or more files as a group for processing. Common file operations can thus be performed on a group of files with a single command.

- *Shell scripts.* A commonly used sequence of shell commands can be stored in a file. The name of the file can later be used to execute the stored sequence with a single command.

- *Shell variables.* The user can control the behavior of the shell, as well as other programs and utilities, by storing data in variables.

- *Programming language constructs.* The shell includes features that allow it to be used as a programming language. These features can be used to build shell scripts that perform complex operations.

Using the Shell

User interaction with the shell takes the form of a dialogue. First, the shell asks the user for input, then the user types a command, and finally the shell causes the command to be carried out. When the command's task has been completed, the shell once again asks the user for input, the user types a command, and so on. When the shell is ready for command input, the shell displays a *prompt* on the terminal screen, usually a *dollar sign* ($). Figure 5.1 shows the sequence of steps in a user's dialogue with the shell.

The shell itself does not carry out most of the commands that are typed to it. Instead, the shell examines each command and starts the appropriate UNIX utility program that carries out the requested action. It is easy for the shell to determine which utility program to start, since the name of the command and the name of the utility program are the same! The standard UNIX system comes with over two hundred utility programs. (One of these utilities is **sh**—the shell itself.)

User programs are started in the same way as the UNIX utilities. The user types the name of the program as a command, and the shell executes the program on the user's behalf.

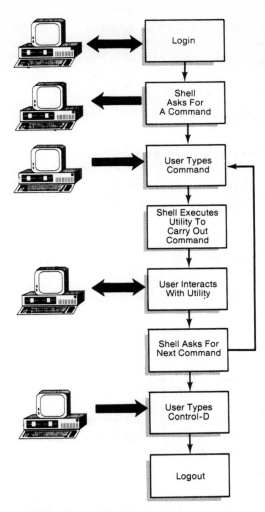

Fig. 5.1. *Using the UNIX Shell*

Shell Commands

All commands typed to the shell have a similar format, shown in Figure 5.2. A command line consists of a sequence of words, each separated by one or more spaces. The first word is the *command* itself, which is the name of the utility or user program to be executed, and which tells the shell "what" to do. The remaining words are command options and arguments. An *option* controls "how" the command is to be performed. An *argument*, usually a file name, indicates on "which" files (or other items) the command will operate. In Figure 5.2, the **ls** utility displays the file names in a directory. The **-l** option requests the long form of the command output. Finally, the **/sales/east/boston** argument tells which directory to look in for the names and information.

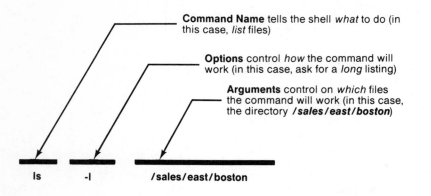

Command Name tells the shell *what* to do (in this case, *list* files)

Options control *how* the command will work (in this case, ask for a *long* listing)

Arguments control on *which* files the command will work (in this case, the directory **/sales/east/boston**)

ls   -l   **/sales/east/boston**

Fig. 5.2. *UNIX Command Structure*

Command Input and Output

Most UNIX utility programs perform one simple, well-defined function. They take some data as input, perform some processing on the data, and produce the results as output. When a user requests execution of a program by typing its name as a shell command, the shell runs the program and assigns to it three standard files:

- A *standard input* file, from which the program takes its input data
- A *standard output* file, which receives the output of the program
- A *standard error* file, which receives any error messages generated during processing

Figure 5.3 illustrates this structure.

Normally, the shell launches a program with all three of its standard files automatically assigned to the user's terminal. When the program requests input, it comes from the terminal keyboard. When the program produces output or error messages, they appear on the terminal display. Figure 5.4 shows the assignment of the standard input, output, and error files to the terminal.

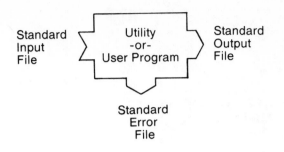

Fig. 5.3. *Standard Files*

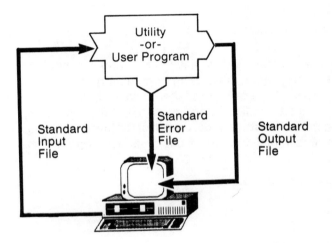

Fig. 5.4. *Standard File Assignments*

Input/Output Redirection

One of the most powerful features of the shell is its ability to reassign the standard input and output files of a command. This capability is known as input and output *redirection*. For example, suppose a program named **in-quiry** takes a list of one or more customer numbers as its input and presents data from a customer master file as its output. Normally, the program will take its input from the terminal and display its output on the screen, as in the following example:

```
$ inquiry
12345

Customer #:      12345
Name:            Consolidated Industries
Address:         1234 Chestnut St.
City:            Maintown
State:           CA
Zip:             Ø1234
Balance:         $22,126.78
   .
   .
   .
```

If the **inquiry** program is to be executed for a list of a hundred customers, typing the customer numbers, one by one, as input to the **inquiry** program would be tedious and might introduce errors. Alternatively, the list of customer numbers can be placed in a file, using one of the UNIX text-editing utilities. The user can then *redirect* the standard input of the **inquiry** program to this file. If the file **numbers** contains the list of customer numbers, then the command

```
$ inquiry <numbers
   .
   .
   .
```

will generate the customer information for the list of customers. The *less than sign* (<) instructs the shell to launch the **inquiry** program, taking its standard input from the file **numbers** rather than the terminal keyboard.

Similarly, the output of a program can be redirected to a file other than the terminal display. The command

```
$ inquiry > /dev/lp
   .
   .
   .
```

causes the **inquiry** program to take its customer numbers from the terminal keyboard, but to display its output on the printer (named **/dev/lp**) rather than the terminal display. The *greater than sign* (>) instructs the shell to redirect the standard output of the **inquiry** program.

Both the standard input and output files of a program can be redirected at the same time, as in the following command:

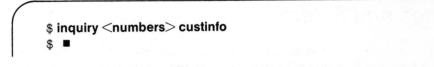

```
$ inquiry <numbers> custinfo
$ ■
```

In this case, the **inquiry** program takes its input from the file named **numbers** and sends its output to the file named **custinfo**. Figure 5.5 graphically illustrates the effects of I/O redirection.

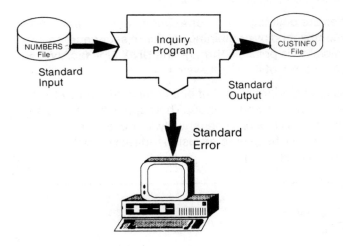

Fig. 5.5. *I/O Redirection with the Shell*

Output redirected to a file normally causes existing contents of the file to be overwritten. However, output can be added to the end of a file by using two adjacent greater than signs (>>) in place of the >. There are a number of other variations to the redirection facility of the shell, but their uses are beyond the scope of this book.

Recall that a major feature of the UNIX file system is file and device independence. Combined with the shell's input/output redirection capability, this feature becomes even more powerful. With file and device independence, any program written to process data from one type of file or device can be used with other files and devices *without changing the program*.

The user can choose the actual files or input/output devices to be used by a program just before the program is run. This selection opportunity greatly increases the flexibility of the utilities and the user programs running on the UNIX system.

Pipes and Filters

Many useful UNIX utilities are designed to accept data from a single input file, process the data, and present the results on a single output file. Such a program is known as a *filter*. Like a mechanical filter, a UNIX filter selectively alters the data flowing through it. For example, the UNIX utility **dd** can be used as a filter to take an input file containing upper- and lowercase text and produce an output file with only uppercase text.

Generally, UNIX utilities are built to perform one simple function well. More complex tasks are accomplished by combining utilities in sequence, one after the other. This combining is possible through the UNIX pipe facility, one of the most celebrated features of the UNIX system.

A *pipe* is used to pass the standard output of one command directly to another command, to be used as its standard input. This capability is especially useful when two commands will be run sequentially. For example, a sorted list of customer information can be generated, using redirection, with the following sequence of commands:

```
$ sort numbers >tempfile
$ inquiry <tempfile
    .
    .
    .
```

The **sort** command sorts the customer numbers for the inquiry and places the sorted list of numbers in a temporary file named **tempfile**. The **inquiry** program then takes its input from the temporary file and produces the customer information on the terminal display.

Alternatively, the same output can be generated without the use of a temporary file by using the pipe facility:

$ **sort numbers** | **inquiry**

    .
    .
    .

The *vertical bar* (|) is the pipe character, instructing the shell to "pipe" the output of the **sort** command directly to the inquiry program as its input. Figure 5.6 illustrates the preceding example.

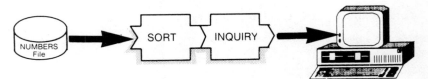

Fig. 5.6. *The UNIX Pipe Feature*

Note what has occurred here. Two simple programs, which had not been specifically written to work together, have been combined to form a "sorted-inquiry" function. This new function was created without writing any new programs. The ability to make new functions out of existing functions is a major benefit of the pipe facility.

With this facility, the shell allows any number of commands to be connected in a sequence, known as a *pipeline.* As in the example above, the standard output of each command in the sequence (except the last) is "piped into" the standard input of the next command. Figure 5.7 illustrates the pipeline concept. All of the programs in a pipeline execute at the same time. UNIX automatically handles the data flow from one program to the next, producing the same effect as if one large program, rather than several smaller ones, had been executed.

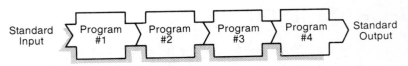

Fig. 5.7. *A UNIX Pipeline*

The UNIX system includes many file-processing utilities that can be used as filters. Utilities are available to select lines from a file, sort the lines into order, reformat the lines, etc. By combining these utilities into pipelines, most file-processing functions can be performed without writing new programs.

Pipe Fitting

Generally, the intermediate output files of a pipeline are of no use outside the pipeline. The kernel simply discards the files' contents after the pipeline has finished its work. The **tee** utility is used to preserve an intermediate output file from within a pipeline, for later processing. Figure 5.8 shows how **tee** operates. It copies each line from the standard input file to the standard output file, but it also copies the line to one or more other files, identified by name. Thus, the pipeline

$ **sort numbers** | **tee tempfile** | **inquiry**
  .
  .
  .

preserves the sorted list of customer numbers from the previous example in a file named **tempfile**.

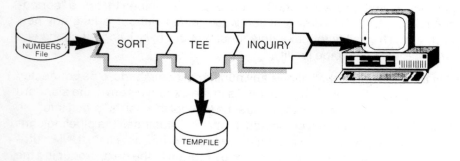

Fig. 5.8. *Pipe Fitting with the TEE Utility*

Wild-Card Matching

Users of a UNIX system often need to perform a file-processing operation on an entire group of files. For example, a user may want to remove all the files in a certain directory. Or perhaps all the files that relate to forecasting have names beginning with the letters "fore" and must be copied to another directory for processing. The shell allows a user to perform these operations on a group of files, with a single command, through the shell's "wild card" matching facility.

The shell interprets two characters as *wild cards*. When these characters are used in a file name as part of a shell command line, they are interpreted in a special way. The *asterisk* (*) matches any sequence of zero or more characters in a file name. The *question mark* (?) matches exactly one character. A few examples illustrate this concept clearly.

If the user wanted to delete all the files in the current directory, the following command would achieve this effect:

```
$ rm *
$ ■
```

Since the asterisk matches any number of characters in a file name, the asterisk matches all the file names in the directory (all of which contain from one to fourteen characters). Similarly, the command

```
$ rm fore*
$ ■
```

will remove all file names that begin with the four characters "fore." Files named **forecast**, **forecast1**, **forecast10**, and **fore** will be removed, whereas files named **oldforecast** or **for** will not be removed.

For single character matching, the question mark wild-card character is used. For example, the command

```
$ rm forecast?
$ ■
```

will remove the files named **forecast1** and **forecastx**, but not the file named **forecast** or the file named **forecast10**, since the question mark must match exactly one character.

The shell offers a more precise kind of wild-card matching that resembles the matching behavior of the question mark, but restricts the characters that will be matched. A list of characters enclosed in *square brackets* ([ ]) will match any one of the designated characters. For example, the command

```
$ rm forecast[123]
$ ■
```

will remove files named **forecast1**, **forecast2**, and **forecast3**, but will not remove a file named **forecast5** or **forecast**. The same effect can also be achieved with a range of characters, instead of a list, as in the following:

```
$ rm  forecast[1-3]
$ ■
```

Wild-card characters can be intermixed with regular characters in a file name, such as **for??ast[13]**. All the wild-card-matching features can be used any time that a file name appears in a shell command. Wild-card matching provides a convenient way to manipulate groups of files as a unit.

Background Processing

Normally, the dialogue between the user and the UNIX shell, and between the user and the UNIX utilities, happens interactively. A user initiates only one activity at a time, and the shell waits until the activity is complete before prompting the user for the next command.

Some time-consuming tasks do not require interaction with the user. These include long-running report programs or programs that perform end-of-month update functions. Executing these tasks interactively would tie up a user terminal unnecessarily. To eliminate this problem, a user may request *background* execution (processing) of a time-consuming task. The shell will launch the program and then prompt the user immediately for the next command. In this way, the user may continue with other work while the task is being performed.

A user requests background execution of a program by placing an *ampersand* (**&**) at the end of a command line. For example, the following command will run the **inquiry** program *in the background*, sending its output to the printer:

```
$ inquiry <numbers> /dev/lp &
4567
$ ■
```

The shell displays an identifying number for the background task and then prompts for the next command. The user is immediately free to type another command and to execute additional programs while the background program continues to execute. By requesting background execution over and over again, a user can cause the UNIX system to work on several tasks at once. Figure 5.9 illustrates background processing.

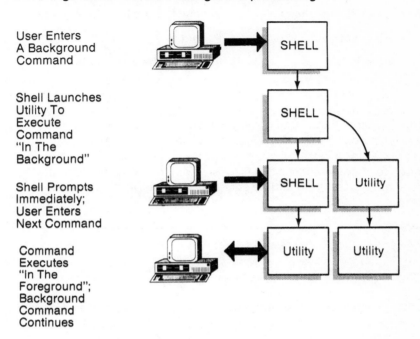

User Enters
A Background
Command

Shell Launches
Utility To
Execute
Command
"In The
Background"

Shell Prompts
Immediately;
User Enters
Next Command

Command
Executes
"In The
Foreground";
Background
Command
Continues

Fig. 5.9. *Background Processing*

Shell Scripts

Most UNIX system users find that they use the same sequences of shell commands over and over again. These command sequences can be stored in a file called a *shell script*. The entire sequence of commands in the script can then be executed simply by typing the name of the file as a command to the shell.

For example, suppose that sales results for each week of the month are stored in files named **week1**, **week2**, **week3**, and **week4**. The usual procedure at the end of each month is to combine the weekly results into a single file, named **results**, for the month. A monthly sales report is printed, and the weekly sales files are then removed.

The following sequence of four shell commands accomplishes the end-of-month procedure for the Boston office:

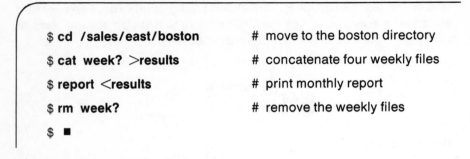

```
$ cd /sales/east/boston        # move to the boston directory
$ cat week? >results           # concatenate four weekly files
$ report <results              # print monthly report
$ rm week?                     # remove the weekly files
$ ■
```

The same four commands can be typed each month, but this kind of repetitive typing can be avoided with shell scripts. Using one of the standard UNIX text editors, the user can prepare a four-line file containing the sequence of commands. If this file were named **endmonth**, then the end-of-month procedure could be accomplished simply by giving the command

```
$ endmonth
$ ■
```

The shell will examine the file **endmonth** and execute the commands stored there, one after another, just as if they had been typed at the terminal keyboard. The shell prompts the user for the next command only after all the commands in the script have been executed. All the facilities of the shell, including wild-card matching and background processing, can be used within shell scripts.

Notice that the UNIX user invokes a shell script and a UNIX application program in exactly the same way—by typing the name of the file containing the script or program in response to the shell prompt. The shell automatically examines the contents of the named file, determines whether it is a script or program, and executes it appropriately. If the file contains a script, the script's commands are executed under control of the shell; if the file contains a program, the program is loaded and executed under control of the shell. Thus, an application designer can freely intermix shell scripts and "real" programs in an application. The application user sees no difference between them.

Shell Variables

Simple shell scripts can be used as convenient typing aids, since they replace an entire sequence of command lines with a single command typed by the user. However, this use of shell scripts is also inflexible, since the sequence of commands will be executed exactly the same way each time the script is invoked. As a result, ten different shell scripts would be required to run the end-of-month procedure for each of ten sales offices.

Shell scripts can be made more flexible by using a feature of the shell called shell variables. A *shell variable* is a name that is used to store a string of characters. The *value* of the variable is the character string. Like file names, variable names can be any sequence of characters, and the names are usually chosen to describe the kind of information the variables store. For example, a variable named **OFFICE** might be used to store the name of a particular sales office. The value of the variable might be "boston" or "newyork."

A variable is assigned a value by typing the variable's name, followed by an *equal sign* (=), followed by the value. Typing

```
$ OFFICE=boston
$ ■
```

to the shell gives the value "boston" to the variable named **OFFICE**.

The value of a variable can later be retrieved for use in a shell command. A *dollar sign* (**$**) followed by a variable name instructs the shell to substitute the value of the variable in place of the variable name before executing the command. For example, the command

```
$ cd /sales/east/$OFFICE
$ ■
```

will make **/sales/east/boston** the current working directory. Before executing the **cd** command, the shell substitutes the value "boston" for the variable named **OFFICE**. The net effect of the command is the same as if the user had typed the following:

```
cd /sales/east/boston
```

Shell variables are especially useful in shell scripts, allowing the script behavior to vary, based on the value of one or more variables. The **endmonth** script in the example earlier can be made more flexible with shell variables. The following modified script can be used to perform the end-of-month pro-

cedure for *any* of the sales offices, depending on the value of the variable
OFFICE:

```
cd /sales/east/$OFFICE   # move to the $OFFICE directory

cat week? >results       # concatenate four weekly files

report <results          # print monthly report

rm week?                 # remove the weekly files
```

This procedure can be performed for the New York sales office, for
example, with these commands:

```
$ OFFICE=newyork
$ export OFFICE
$ endmonth
$ ■
```

The **export** command simply makes the value of the variable **OFFICE** available to the **endmonth** script. With the use of shell variables, the script has
been made more general, and the need for a different script for each office
has been eliminated.

Special Shell Variables

By convention, the UNIX system stores in shell variables several important
pieces of information, which vary from user to user. For example, the shell
finds it convenient to know the name of a user's home directory. Other programs may need to know the kind of terminal being used. Table 5.1 lists
some of the special variables used by the shell and other UNIX utilities.

The special shell variable **PATH** controls which program or utility is executed when a user types a command to the shell. The **PATH** variable holds
a particular sequence of directory names. When the user types a command,
the shell searches these directories, in the order named in the **PATH** variable, to find the utility or user program with the same name as the command
name and to execute it. The sequence of directory names is known as a

Table 5.1
Special Shell Variables

PATH	A list of directories to be searched by the shell to find programs whose names are typed as commands
LOGNAME	The user's name
TERM	The kind of terminal being used
HOME	The name of the user's home directory
MAIL	The name of the user's mailbox for the UNIX mail facility
PS1	The string that is used by the shell to prompt for the next command (usually "**$**")

search path. A typical search path might include the following three directory names:

PATH = :/bin:/usr/bin:/sales/programs

The colons in the search path separate the directory names in the list. Recall that most standard UNIX commands are simply the names of utility programs. By convention, the utilities are stored in the directories named **/bin** and **/usr/bin**. These directories will be included by most UNIX users in their search paths, to instruct the shell to look there automatically for UNIX commands.

With search paths, the names of user programs stored in other directories can also be typed to the shell as commands. For example, if the **endmonth** script were stored in the directory **/sales/programs**, then the inclusion of this directory in the search path allows the user to type **endmonth** as a shell command. The shell will successfully find the script and execute it. Since each user may have a different search path, each user can create a personalized set of commands.

The Shell as a Programming Language

In addition to its role as an interactive command interpreter, the shell can be used as a powerful programming language. Two of its programming language features have already been described—shell scripts and shell variables. Many such programming language features are available, allowing users to create sophisticated scripts that accomplish complex tasks. These features include the following:

- *Scripts.* A sequence of commands can be stored in a file for later execution.

- *Variables.* Values stored in named variables can be used within shell scripts.

- *Arguments.* Data can be passed to variables within a shell script by typing the values as arguments on the command line.

- *Conditional execution.* The sequence of executed commands can be varied, based on some external condition. (**if . . . then . . . else** command)

- *Case selection.* One of several alternative command sequences can be selected for execution, based on some external condition. (**case** command)

- *Repetition.* A sequence of commands can be executed repeatedly for a list of values, each time assigning the next value to a shell variable. (**for** command)

- *Conditional repetition.* A sequence of commands can be executed repeatedly until some external condition occurs. (**while** command)

- *Command substitution.* The standard output of a command in a script may be redirected into the script itself, becoming part of another command.

- *Comments.* Descriptive text can be included in a shell script to help explain its operation.

An Example of a Shell Script

The shell's programming language constructs are normally used by sophisticated UNIX users with some programming background. Shell scripts are often used in place of actual programs written in languages like BASIC, C, or Pascal. In fact, several UNIX system utilities are actually sophisticated shell scripts. Figure 5.10 shows a relatively simple shell script that uses programming constructs.

The **for** command in the script causes the sequence of commands between the **do** and **done** commands to be executed once for each office. When the sequence of commands is executed, the value of the shell variable **OFFICE** will be "newyork," then "boston," and then "phila." The command sequence executed for each office is unchanged from the previous end-of-month procedure. The **echo** commands display informational messages on the ter-

```
# This script performs the end-of-month procedure for each
# sales office in the eastern region.
#
for OFFICE in newyork boston phila          # For each office . . .
   do
   cd  /sales/east/$OFFICE                  # move to the correct
                                            # directory . . .
   cat  week? >results                      # perform  the
   report <results                          # end-of-month
   rm  week?                                # procedure . . .
   echo  Finished with  $OFFICE             # . . . and print a
                                            # message.
   done
echo  All  sales reports  complete          # Indicate when
                                            # complete.
```

Fig. 5.10. *A Shell Script with Programming Constructs*

minal screen as the script executes. All text following the *pound sign* (#) on each line of the script is a comment, which is ignored by the shell.

Utilities for Building Shell Scripts

Several shell utilities are especially useful for constructing shell scripts. For example, it is often useful to have a script display messages on the terminal screen as the script executes. Or a script may need to test the value of a shell variable or check to see whether a required file is present before trying to use it. Table 5.2 lists the utilities that perform these and other functions which are particularly useful for script building.

User Aids

The shell includes many powerful features and can be intimidating for new UNIX users. In addition, the UNIX commands tend to have cryptic names and obscure single-letter command options. To simplify the task of learning how to use UNIX, the system offers two tools: a help facility and the **ASSIST** utility.

Table 5.2
Useful Utilities for Building Shell Scripts

echo	Displays a prompt or message on the standard output file
read	Reads values from the standard input file into shell variables
test	Tests for various conditions, such as the existence of a file; useful for controlling conditional script execution
expr	Evaluates an expression and outputs its value
true	Returns a *true* value; useful for condition testing
false	Returns a *false* value; useful for condition testing
wait	Waits for the completion of background processing; is used to ensure that critical processing is complete before proceeding in a script
sleep	Causes command execution to stop for a specified number of seconds

The help facility provides on-line access to basic information about how to use the system when the user enters the **help** command. The available information includes

- Starter information for the UNIX beginner, describing basic use of UNIX from an interactive terminal

- A glossary of technical terms to help users understand unfamiliar words or concepts

- Suggestions for the UNIX commands that perform certain functions, based on one or more user-supplied keywords that describe the function

- Information about the proper syntax and usage of each UNIX command and utility

With the companion help-facility administration utility, **helpadm**, a system manager can customize the help facility for a particular installation. For example, installation-specific terms can be added to the glossary, and information about command usage can be expanded to support installation-specific utilities.

ASSIST is a menu-driven, forms-based utility that helps the user construct UNIX commands. Although **ASSIST** can be viewed as an alternative shell, one of **ASSIST**'s primary purposes is to teach the user about UNIX commands and options. **ASSIST** begins operation by offering a top-level menu of UNIX operations, arranged topically. Selecting a topic (such as "File Operations") leads to a lower-level topical menu or to a menu of UNIX commands containing one-sentence explanations of every command.

When the user selects a specific command, **ASSIST** displays a form that must be filled in to specify the command options. For example, the form for the **cp** (copy a file) command prompts for the names of the source and destination files. Other prompts request information about command options; these prompts often can be answered with a simple yes/no choice. As the user responds to the prompts in the form, **ASSIST** builds the corresponding command line at the bottom of the screen. In this way, as users gain experience with the command forms, they can begin to enter the proper commands and options directly.

In addition to predefined menus and forms, **ASSIST** includes another utility, **astgen**, for tailoring **ASSIST**. The system manager can use this utility to customize the **ASSIST** menus and forms for a particular installation.

Alternative Shells

Although the Bourne shell is the most widely used user interface for the UNIX system, users are free to use alternative shells. In fact, each user on a UNIX system could have a separate shell with its own unique user interface! Several important alternative shells have been developed, including

- *Restricted shell.* A restricted version of the Bourne shell, used in environments where the operations that can be performed by a user must be restricted for security or other reasons

- *C shell.* A shell developed as part of the Berkeley UNIX versions and popular with C programmers because the command structure resembles that of the C programming language

- *Visual shell.* An end-user-oriented shell offered as part of XENIX, which offers a menu-driven user interface patterned after the MultiPlan spreadsheet

The Restricted Shell

The restricted shell, **rsh**, is a restricted version of the Bourne shell. The restricted shell is used typically in secure installations where users must be restricted to work only in their own limited environments. The following restrictions are imposed by the restricted shell:

- The user cannot move out of the current working directory; access to other parts of the file system is cut off.

- The user cannot change the **$PATH** environment variable; execution of programs in directories other than those authorized by the system manager is prevented.

- The user cannot specify absolute path names beginning at the root; again, access to other parts of the file system is cut off.

- The user cannot redirect input or output.

By setting up the system so that a user encounters the restricted shell when logging in, the system manager can effectively limit the tasks that can be performed by that user and so enhance the security of the system.

The C Shell

The C shell (**csh**) was originally offered as part of the Berkeley version of UNIX. This shell is very similar to the Bourne shell; in fact, most of the commands are exactly the same in both shells. But the C shell also includes several built-in "convenience" features that make it a very efficient tool for expert UNIX users.

One of the C shell's most powerful capabilities is its *history list* feature. The C shell automatically saves the commands that a user types, to form a *command history*. The user can display this history and also reuse commands or parts of commands through a shorthand notation. The *exclamation point* character (!), when typed to the C shell, invokes the history feature. The characters immediately following the exclamation point control which part of the command history will be reused.

For example, typing

```
% !c
%
```

causes the C shell to reexecute the most recent command that began with the letter *c*. Note that the percent sign (%) is the C shell prompt. Similarly, the command

```
% !!
%
```

causes the C shell to repeat the last command. The user can also reuse just the arguments of a previous command. In the example

```
% ls  text1  text2
text1
text2
% cat !*
.
.
.
```

the user first confirms with the **ls** command that two files are in the current directory, then displays their contents with the **cat** command. The !* characters instruct the C shell to reuse the file list, thus saving keystrokes.

The shorthand capabilities of the history mechanism are much more sophisticated than these examples demonstrate. Using the C shell, a user can isolate individual words of a previous command for reuse and even edit a previous command before reusing it. Although the history mechanism may appear confusing to the novice, in the hands of an experienced user, the mechanism can save considerable typing. This is especially true in software development applications, where the same sequence of commands is often repeated over and over.

Another useful C shell feature is its **alias** facility. With this feature, the user can give a command or a phrase an *alias*—a single word that will be used as an abbreviation. For example, a PC DOS user accustomed to using the **dir** command to list file names might establish the following alias:

```
% alias  dir  ls  -l
% ■
```

Once the alias has been established, the C shell automatically substitutes the full command or phrase every time the alias appears in a command typed to it. The **unalias** command deletes aliases that are no longer needed.

The C shell provides a protection against accidentally overwriting existing files. When the shell variable **noclobber** is set on, the C shell will prevent the standard output from being redirected to an already existing file. The C shell also supports shell scripts, but the commands that control the flow of script execution are somewhat different from those of the Bourne shell. The C shell flow control commands resemble the corresponding constructs in the C programming language, hence, the name C shell.

The Visual Shell

The visual shell (**vsh**) is a menu-driven interface offered as part of the XENIX system, to simplify its operation for end-users. Both the Bourne shell and the C shell require that a user know the names of the UNIX commands in advance—the shells simply display a prompt, and the user must type a valid command. In contrast, the visual shell presents the user with a menu of choices. The user always knows what options are available at any time and simply chooses one of them.

The user interface of the visual shell resembles that of the PC applications packages available from Microsoft, such as Multiplan. The visual shell uses a full-screen display, as shown in Figure 5.11.

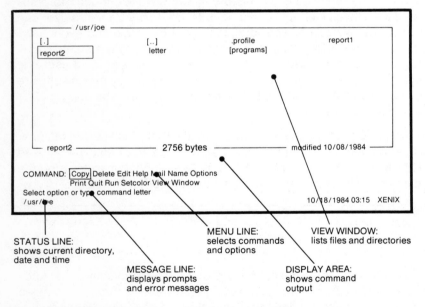

Fig. 5.10. *A Shell Script with Programming Constructs*

To use the visual shell, the user chooses a command from the menu line. The space bar moves the cursor from choice to choice, and the return key makes the selection. As a shortcut, typing the first letter of a command automatically selects a menu choice. Once a command has been selected, more menus may be displayed, offering a choice of command options.

For commands that use files, the view window provides an easy way to se-lect specific files for processing. A list of the currently available files is al-ways displayed in the view window, and the cursor keys on the keyboard move within the list for selection.

The view window can also be used for conveniently browsing the contents of files and directories. Pressing the equal sign (=) key causes the visual shell to "zoom in" on the contents of the selected file or directory. Zooming in on a directory displays a list of the files contained in the directory; zooming in on a file displays its contents. Pressing the minus sign (–) key zooms back out of the previous viewing level.

The visual shell's command menus provide access to the most frequently used UNIX commands for file management, text processing, and electronic mail. More advanced UNIX commands are available through the **RUN** menu selection, which allows the user to type the name of any UNIX command or shell script.

The Shell Layer Manager

In some situations, the user needs to interact with several programs in par-allel, switching back and forth between them as required. For example, a manager using a word-processing program to compose a memo may oc-casionally want to switch to a spreadsheet program to compute results and to a report-viewing program to see a summary of other data. The shell layer manager (**shl**) is a utility that supports this kind of parallel interaction with several programs.

The layer manager provides parallel processing by allowing the user to in-teract with more than one shell from a single terminal. Each shell started by the layer manager is called a *layer*, and each layer processes in parallel with other layers, as shown in Figure 5.12. Each layer is identified by a distinct name assigned when the layer is created. When running programs under the layer manager, the user typically is working in one of the layers, identified as the *current layer*; keyboard input by the user is received by this layer.

While the user is interacting with the current layer, the other layers may con-tinue processing in parallel. If another layer tries to read input from the ter-minal, however, that layer is blocked until the user makes it the current layer. To allow noncurrent layers to notify the user of important events, output from the other layers is not blocked. A program completing a long calculation, for example, can alert the user by displaying a message on the terminal. The

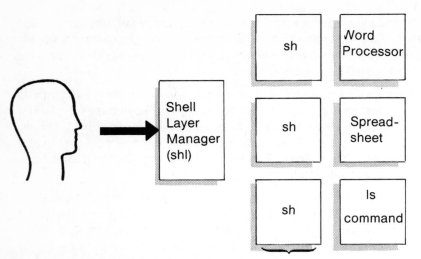

Fig. 5.12. *The Shell Layer Manager*

user sees the message even if the sending program is not running in the current layer.

In addition to creating the environment for running programs in parallel, the layer manager provides commands that

- Create a new layer and enter it
- Delete a layer
- List the name and status of each layer
- Switch to a different layer
- Block output of a noncurrent layer, to prevent the output from destroying a screen display

These commands give the user an effective job-control facility for managing multiple layers.

Batch Processing

Sometimes, noninteractive tasks must be performed on a scheduled basis. For example, nightly file backup or transmission of inventory status data to another system may be required at scheduled times. Other tasks have no specific time associated with them but are performed as the system's workload permits. The UNIX utilities **at** and **batch** support these modes of processing.

The **at** utility runs the sequence of commands provided on its standard input at a later time, specified on the command line. Usually, the standard input is redirected to a file containing a sequence of commands, as in the following examples:

```
$ at 8:15am<cmdfile        # run cmdfile at 8:15am
1154
$ at 5pm friday<cmdfile     # run cmdfile at 5pm on friday
1161
$ at now + 2 day<cmdfile    # run cmdfile two days from now
1166
```

As the examples show, **at** provides many different ways to specify the time to run the commands. Because the user may no longer be logged into the system when the commands are run, the standard output and standard error files from the command execution are mailed to the user. In addition to scheduling jobs for execution, other options of the **at** command allow a user to see a list of previously scheduled jobs and to cancel them by number.

The system manager can selectively permit or deny access to the **at** utility on a user-by-user basis by including user names in control files associated with the utility.

The **batch** command works like the **at** utility, taking from its standard input a sequence of commands for later execution. However, the **batch** facility does not execute the commands at a specific time. Instead, **batch** schedules execution of the commands as the system's workload permits.

CHAPTER

6

Multiuser Operation

UNIX is a multiuser operating system by design. Multiuser capabilities were incorporated into the system very soon after its creation to support programming groups that needed a shared system for software development. Today, UNIX systems are used by as few as one or as many as a hundred simultaneous users, and UNIX supports diverse applications, such as

- *Software development.* A group of programmers can use UNIX software development tools to develop their own programs, while sharing common modules, such as file definitions and subroutines.

- *Text processing.* A group of writers can use UNIX text-processing tools to prepare individual sections of a single document, such as an administrative manual or a technical manuscript.

- *Applications processing.* In a small business, clerical personnel can use a system for accounting, inventory control, and order-processing tasks and can share common data among the departments.

This chapter describes the UNIX features and commands that support multiuser operation.

91

Multiuser Features and Benefits

The major UNIX system features that support multiuser operation are the following:

- *Multiprocessing.* UNIX supports multiple users through concurrent execution of multiple programs. Individual users may also execute multiple programs concurrently.

- *System security.* A user password scheme controls access to the UNIX system.

- *File security.* Access to UNIX files is controlled on a user-by-user basis; three different forms of file access can be selectively allowed or disallowed.

- *Spooling.* UNIX system utilities manage shared access to printers by multiple users.

- *Accounting.* UNIX monitors usage of system resources and maintains accounting records.

- *System administration.* UNIX provides utilities for system maintenance and administration functions, such as backup and error recovery.

The Concept of a Process

The fundamental unit of multiuser UNIX operation is the *process.* Simply stated, a process is a program in a state of execution. When a user runs a program on the UNIX system, the running program is called a process. We speak of processes "doing things," as in "this process is printing checks on the printer," or "this process will open three files and merge their contents." A process is a program doing useful work on a UNIX system.

UNIX supports multiple users by allowing multiple processes to execute concurrently. A small, desktop UNIX system may have as many as ten processes in execution at one time. A large UNIX system, supporting several dozen users, may have over a hundred processes in concurrent execution. UNIX uses processes liberally. Almost nothing gets done in a UNIX system without creating a process to perform the task.

Of course, most UNIX systems have only one central processor; therefore, the system can actually be working on only one process at a time. The system creates the illusion of serving many users simultaneously by switching the CPU—very rapidly—from one process to the next. Because a typical UNIX system executes hundreds of thousands of instructions each second, the CPU can make quite a bit of progress on each user's work, even during a short period of time.

User Names

A typical UNIX system may have as many as a hundred different users. Each authorized user of the system is identified by a unique *user name*, containing up to eight characters. First names, last names, and job titles are often used as user names. UNIX uses the user name in several different ways. Accounting reports that show system usage are frequently sorted by user name. Utilities that list the people currently working on the system will display a list of user names. One of the most important functions of user names is to aid in implementing system and file security.

Because UNIX finds it easier to deal with numbers than with names, each user name corresponds to a unique user number known as a *user-id*, which is used internally within UNIX. User-id's sometimes appear in place of user names in UNIX reports and command output. The system administrator maintains the list of authorized user names, which is stored, along with other important information about each user, in the file **/etc/passwd**.

User Groups

Each UNIX system user may be a member of one or more *user groups* known to the system. User groups are usually comprised of users with related job functions or with similar needs for access to data. For example, in a small company, order-processing clerks may comprise one group; accounting clerks, another group; and the accounting supervisors who generate monthly reports, yet another group. Normally, the system administrator maintains the list of groups and group memberships, which is kept in the file **/etc/group**. User groups form a part of the UNIX file security scheme.

A user group is identified by a name, containing up to eight characters. Again, the system finds it more convenient to deal internally with the corresponding *group-id* number. A typical user group arrangement is illustrated in Figure 6.1. As the figure shows, a user may be a member of more than one group. However, membership can be *active* in only one group at any one time. A UNIX utility is used to change the active group membership from one group to another.

Marketing Group   Accounting Group

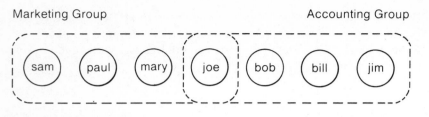

Fig. 6.1. *User Names and User Groups*

UNIX Security

One of the key concerns on any multiuser computer system is the security of both the system and the data stored in it. Therefore, good security and protection features are much more important in the UNIX system than in personal computer operating systems.

Security in a personal computer is generally easy to maintain. Simply locking away the computer and the floppy disks that contain private data is usually adequate. In contrast, the data on a typical UNIX system is stored on a nonremovable disk. The system will have many attached terminals scattered throughout a building. Dial-in lines may also permit access from terminals in other locations. Thus, physical security of a UNIX system is difficult to maintain. In addition, the data stored on a typical UNIX system belongs to many individual users who expect their data to be kept private, even from other authorized users of the system.

UNIX concentrates its security features at the following two levels:

- *System level security.* UNIX restricts access to the system to only authorized users through a login/logout scheme.

- *File level security.* UNIX provides privacy for stored data through a file access permission scheme.

Logging In

UNIX implements system level security through its *login* procedure. Before granting access to the system, UNIX requests a user name from the prospective user, then checks the reply against the list of authorized user names. UNIX grants access to the system only if the name is found in the list.

In addition, UNIX provides an extra measure of security by allowing each user to have a password associated with the user's name. Without passwords, security of a UNIX system would be very low since the names of authorized users may be well known to others seeking access. If a user name is password-protected, the login procedure will demand both the user name and the corresponding password from the prospective user. To minimize the risk of a password being accidentally revealed, UNIX turns off the display of typed characters on the terminal screen while the user types the password. A typical login sequence is included in Figure 6.2.

```
login: joe
Password:

/***********************************/
  Welcome to the Sales Dept System
/***********************************/
you have mail

$ pwd
/sales/east/boston
$ ls
forecast
orders
personnel
results
$ cat forecast
Smith    $10,654      12/83    Acme Fish Market
Smith    $ 2,450      11/83    John's Hardware
Harris   $13,295      10/83    Wayland Distributing
Harris   $ 4,270      11/83    Wayland Distributing
Jones    $ 2,235      10/83    Central Transportation
$
login:
```

Fig. 6.2. *A Short UNIX Session*

UNIX stores encrypted the corresponding user names, in the **/etc/passwd** file. When the user types a password during the login sequence, the characters typed are encrypted, and the result is compared against the stored encrypted password for the user. Thus, security derives primarily from the complex encryption method used and from the user's ability to change passwords frequently by using a UNIX utility program.

Logging Out

Once a user has logged in to the system, the user's work session continues until the user instructs the shell to terminate the session. A user *logs out* by typing the *end-of-file* character (**Control-D**) to the shell, instead of typing a command. The system displays the `login:` prompt on the terminal display and awaits login by the next user.

File Access Permissions

UNIX implements a second level of security to protect a user's files against unauthorized access by other users of the system. Each file and directory in a UNIX system has exactly one user who is the *owner* of the file. The owner is typically the user who originally created the file. Each file also has a *group owner*, which is one of the user groups on the system.

In addition to information about the file's ownership, a set of *file access permissions* is maintained for each file and directory. These permissions determine which users may access the file and what kinds of file access will be permitted.

The following three types of file access can be granted or denied:

- *Read access* allows examination of a file's contents. The file may be displayed on a terminal, copied, compiled, etc., if a user has read access to it.

- *Write access* allows both modifying a file's contents and adding information to the file. The file may be altered or deleted if a user has write access to it.

- *Execute access* allows execution of a file as a program.

Each of these three types of file access may be selectively granted or denied to the following three different classes of users:

- The *owner* of the file

- Users in the *group owner* of the file

- *Other users* of the system

Figure 6.3 illustrates the nine file access permissions (three types of access for each of three classes of users) that are available for each file. Permissions offer a fair amount of flexibility in establishing file security. For example, in a small business, the company controller might be granted read and write access to the personnel file, whereas the accounting clerks, as a group, have only read access to process payrolls. The rest of the company is denied any access at all. In contrast, the budget report files are open to all users for read access, but can be updated only by clerks in the accounting group. The report programs that generate the budget reports are open to the accounting group for execute access, but no one has write access to these same programs, to prevent accidental destruction.

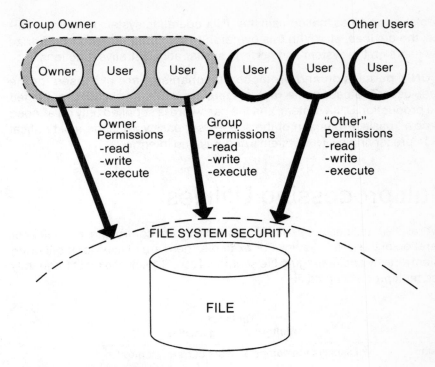

Fig. 6.3. *File System Security*

File access permissions apply also to directories and special files. Read access to a directory allows a user to list the files in the directory. Write access allows a user to add new files to the directory. Finally, execute access to a directory allows a user to make that directory the user's own working directory.

The Super-User

Certain administrative functions on a UNIX system require access to files and commands that are normally denied to all users. Adding a new name to the list of authorized user names is an example of one of these functions. On a multiuser UNIX system, these functions are usually performed by a system administrator, a "special" user charged with maintenance and general operation of the computer system. UNIX provides an exception to its file security scheme for this single user of the system, called the *super-user*.

By convention, the super-user is given the user name **root**. As the name implies, the super-user owns the root directory. The super-user also owns the directories and files that contain the UNIX operating system kernel, the utilities, the devices, etc. With this ownership, the super-user can authorize new users on the system and perform similar administrative functions.

All UNIX permission and protection mechanisms are bypassed for the super-user. The user name **root** is, therefore, always password-protected on a production UNIX system, and the password is supplied only on a "need to know" basis. Protection of the super-user password is the most critical link in preserving a UNIX system's security and integrity.

Multiprocessing Utilities

Several UNIX utilities are useful for monitoring and controlling the multiuser operation of the UNIX system. For example, there are utilities for monitoring system activity and managing file security. Table 6.1 lists the most frequently used multiprocessing utilities.

Table 6.1
Multiprocessing Utilities

who	Displays the names of users currently logged in
ps	Displays process status information
kill	Terminates a process
passwd	Changes a user's password
chown	Changes ownership of a file
chgrp	Changes the group owner of a file
chmod	Changes access permissions of a file
newgrp	Changes a user's active membership to a new group
su	Temporarily changes a user's user-id
date	Displays the current date and time
at	Runs a command at a specified time
man	Displays entries from the on-line manual

Displaying Current Users

The **who** (**who** is on the system) utility displays the names of users currently logged on to a UNIX system, as in this example:

```
$ who
paul        tty7        11:40
jim         tty10        8:30
joe         tty3         2:00
mary        tty12        9:20
sam         tty4         3:08
$ ■
```

A special option to the **who** utility identifies the user who requested the command, as in the following example:

```
$ who am i
jim         tty10        8:30
$ ■
```

Displaying Process Status

Another utility, **ps** (process status), displays information about the individual processes that are executing on the system:

```
$ ps
  PID        TTY         TIME        COMMAND
   64        10          0:24        sh
 1323        10          0:36        report
 1330        10          0:02        ps
$ ■
```

Each active process is identified by a unique number, called its *process-id* (PID). The **ps** utility displays the process-id, the terminal that controls the process, the cumulative execution time for the process, and the name of the command being executed. Options to the **ps** command control whether the utility displays information for only processes owned by the user, for all processes active on the system, and so on. Other options provide more detailed information, such as the state of the process (running, terminated, waiting, etc.) and the user-id of the user who owns the process.

Terminating Processes

Generally, processes are allowed to run to completion. The user can also forcefully terminate a process with the **kill** command:

```
$ kill  4637
$ ■
```

The **kill** command requires the process-id of the process to be terminated. Various options allow the user to send different *signals* to an executing process instead of killing it directly. The process can detect these signals and will usually respond with an orderly shutdown of its operations before terminating.

Changing Passwords

The **passwd** (change **password**) utility allows a user to change the password associated with the user's name. The utility first prompts for the old password, then requests a new password—twice, to prevent typing errors. The new password is encrypted and saved, and it must be subsequently supplied by the user when logging into the system. The **passwd** utility is also used to establish a password for a new user.

Changing File Ownership

Two utilities are used to change the ownership of a file. The **chown** (**ch**ange **own**er) utility reassigns ownership of a file from one user to another. The **chgrp** (**ch**ange **gr**oup owner) performs the same function for the group that owns the file. For example, the command sequence

```
$ chown  joe  report1
$ chgrp  finance  report1
$ ■
```

will make the user named **joe** the owner of the **report1** file and will make the group named **finance** the group owner of the file.

Changing File Access Permissions

The **chmod** (**ch**ange **mod**e) utility changes the file access permissions for a file. Each one of the nine permissions (read, write, and execute for the owner, group owner, and others) can be individually granted or denied with this utility. The simple command

```
$  chmod  +r  report1
$  ■
```

will grant read access (**+r**) to all three classes of users. The more complex example

```
$  chmod  go-w  report1
$  ■
```

will deny write access (**-w**) to users in the group owning the file (**g**), as well as to all other users (**o**). Figure 6.4 shows how permissions are represented by the **ls** command and illustrates an alternative method of specifying file access permissions with the **chmod** utility.

Changing Groups

The **newgrp** (**new** user **group**) utility changes the user's active group membership from one user group to another. Typed by the user named **joe**, the command

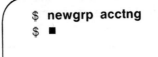

```
$  newgrp  acctng
$  ■
```

will change the user's active group membership to the group named **acctng**. The utility verifies the user's membership in the new group before making it the active group.

Permissions in an LS command:

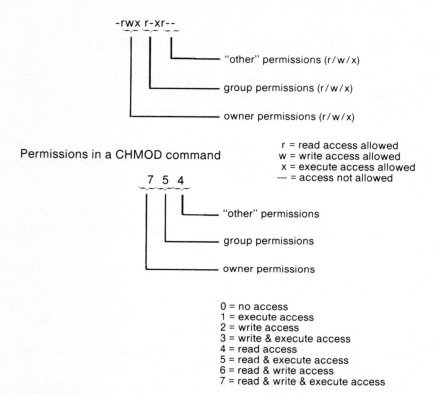

Permissions in a CHMOD command

r = read access allowed
w = write access allowed
x = execute access allowed
— = access not allowed

0 = no access
1 = execute access
2 = write access
3 = write & execute access
4 = read access
5 = read & execute access
6 = read & write access
7 = read & write & execute access

Fig. 6.4. *Representing File Access Permissions*

Changing User-Id's

As a convenience, UNIX provides a utility that allows a user to become another user, without first logging off the system and then logging back in. For example, a user may need temporary access to another user's files and may wish to assume that user's name for a short time. The **su** (become **s**uper **u**ser or another user) utility is used to change the user name (and the corresponding user-id) of a currently logged-in user. For example, if the user named **joe** types the command

```
$ su sam
Password:
$ ▪
```

Joe will temporarily assume the user name **sam** (and its corresponding user-id), and Joe will have access to Sam's files as if Joe had logged in as **sam**. If the new user name has an associated password, the **su** utility requests and validates it. The temporary identity lasts until the user types the end-of-file character to the shell, causing the user to revert back to the user's original user name. The **su** utility is also used to switch to super-user status, by omitting the user name on the command line.

Spooling

In a multiuser environment, access to the system printer(s) must be carefully managed and controlled. Without this control, several users may attempt to send output to a printer at the same time, resulting in intermixed output on the printed pages. *Spooling* is a technique that allows each user to send output to the printer at will, while the system manages the orderly printing of the output.

UNIX includes several spooling utilities that organize multiuser access to one or more printers attached to the system. The utilities operate by copying into temporary disk files the information to be printed. A set of background processes then prints the files, one at a time, on the system printer(s). Figure 6.5 illustrates spooling operation.

The user interface to the UNIX spooling system is the **lp** utility. Under the control of the spooling system, this utility prints standard input. The **lp** utility usually appears as the last program in a pipeline whose final output is to be printed:

```
$ report | sort | lp
$ ▪
```

The **lp** utility can also be used as a command, naming one or more files to be printed on the command line:

```
$ lp report1 report2
$ ▪
```

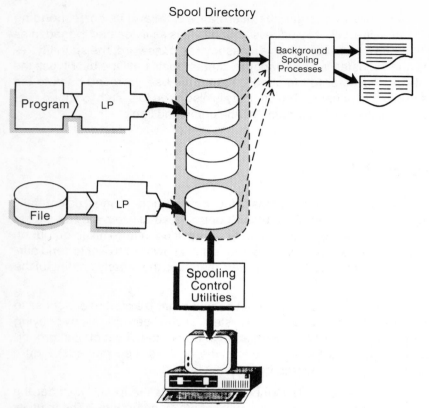

Fig. 6.5. *Spooling Operation (System V)*

The UNIX spooling system includes an entire family of utilities for managing spooling operation. These utilities, along with their functions, are shown in Table 6.2.

The spooling utilities support the following capabilities, which are typically available with most commercial operating systems:

- Requests to print on a specific printer

- Requests to print on a specific class of printer, such as letter-quality or 132-column

- User notification of print completion

- Requests for multicopy printing

- Display of status information for printers and printer classes

- Display of status information for print requests

Table 6.2
Spooling Utilities

lp	Requests printing of files, allowing specification of the number of copies, type of printer to be used, etc.
cancel	Cancels a previous request to print a file
lpstat	Prints the status of printers, lists jobs yet to be printed, etc.
disable	Deactivates a printer
enable	Reactivates a previously deactivated printer
lpadmin	Controls the configuration of spooling printers
accept	Allows spooling requests for a printer
reject	Disallows spooling requests for a printer
lpmove	Moves spooling requests from one printer to another
lpshut	Shuts down the spooling subsystem

- Cancellation of pending print requests
- Cancellation of jobs currently printing

System Administration

In a multiuser computer system, several system administration functions must be performed on a periodic basis to ensure smooth and continued system operation. UNIX includes utilities to support these functions. Accounting utilities permit analysis of system utilization and provide the data for user billing. Backup utilities are used to make backup copies of the system's stored data, to be used later for error recovery. Other utilities play a role in maintaining system integrity.

Multiuser Accounting

The UNIX system optionally records system activity by maintaining a set of system log files. A set of accounting utilities prints reports based on the data in these files. The reports may be used to determine patterns of system use or to identify the need for additional memory, disk storage, terminals, etc. If a system is shared among different departments, the accounting reports can also be used as the basis of a billing scheme that allocates fairly the cost of system operation among the users.

The system maintains two separate log files to support accounting:

- On a *per-process* basis: the system records the name of the program executed, elapsed and CPU-times, main memory usage, and amount of I/O activity. The file also identifies the user-id, the group-id of the process, and the terminal from which the process was started.

- On a *per-login* basis: the system records the user's name, user-id, the CPU-time used, the terminal connect time, the number of processes executed, and disk usage information.

Backup and Recovery

System backup is an important administrative task on a busy multiuser UNIX system. Periodically copying active files from disk to a floppy disk, magnetic tape, or other backup medium protects users against accidental destruction or modification of important files. If an accident does occur, the backup copy of the file can be recovered. The UNIX utility normally used to back up and recover files is **cpio** (**cop**y **in**/**out**). For backup operations, **cpio** reads a list of paths from its standard input; **cpio** copies those files to its standard output, which is normally redirected to the backup device. When restoring files, **cpio** accepts a list of file-name patterns on its command line. The utility searches its standard input, which is normally redirected to the backup device, for files with names matching the patterns and reads these files into the system. Other command options allow the user to print a table of contents for a backup medium, rename files as they are recovered, and control other details of the backup and recovery process.

Another administrative utility is used to verify file system integrity and to repair file systems that have been damaged by system failures. The **fsck** (**f**ile **s**ystem **c**hec**k**) utility checks the directories and file relationships as they appear on the disk and also reports inconsistencies and errors. If the file system does contain errors, **fsck** allows the system administrator to recover as much of the file system as possible. The **fsck** utility is a privileged one that is available only to the super-user.

The UNIX disk buffering scheme presents another opportunity for a loss of data integrity, since data held in the disk buffers may be lost during a system error, such as a power failure. The **sync** (**sync**hronize disk buffers) utility forces the contents of the disk buffers to be written to the disk immediately and not at the convenience of the system. Many installations arrange to have **sync** execute automatically every minute or so, assuring that inconsistencies between the disk and the file buffer are, at most, a minute old. The **sync** utility can be executed by any user.

Table 6.3 summarizes the administrative utilities for system backup and recovery.

Table 6.3
System Backup and Recovery Utilities

cpio	Copies files to and from a backup medium and lists the contents of a backup tape or floppy disk
tar	An older, but still popular, file backup utility, which performs the same functions as **cpio**
fsck	Checks the integrity of file systems and performs repairs
sync	Forces the contents of the disk buffers to be copied to disk
volcopy	Copies a file system to and from a backup device
labelit	Labels an unmounted file system
dcopy	Reorganizes a file system to improve performance

Menu-Driven System Administration

The latest versions of UNIX System V include a menu-driven system administration utility, **sysadmin**, which substantially simplifies the task of UNIX system administration. The utility prompts and guides the user through a series of menus and forms to perform typical system administration tasks, including

- System diagnostics
- Disk management, such as formatting, file system checks, and so on
- File management, such as backup and recovery operations and monitoring disk usage
- System management, including startup and shutdown
- Software management, including installation and deletion of optional software packages
- System setup, such as setting the date, time, and system password
- Terminal management, such as configuring terminal lines

- User management, such as adding and deleting users, groups, and passwords

In addition to entering the **sysadmin** menus from the top level, the system manager can specify command-line options to go directly to a submenu. This capability allows an experienced system manager to have the benefits of a forms-based interface without the overhead of menu selections.

Turnkey Processing with UNIX

The UNIX system offers applications designers an excellent set of facilities for building turnkey applications systems. A turnkey system presents a user with an environment of familiar menus, forms, and application-oriented choices that make an application very easy to use. The user simply "turns the key" to start the system and is prompted and guided through a set of choices specific to the application. Once a turnkey application has been developed, UNIX can become an "invisible foundation" on top of which the application executes. The application user does not have to understand the UNIX system below, or even be aware of it.

This chapter describes the process management facilities of the UNIX system that make it well suited for turnkey applications processing. The chapter also describes some of the UNIX implementation techniques that make UNIX a particularly good foundation for building turnkey systems. Some of this latter information will be of interest only to applications designers. Nontechnical readers should feel free to skip these sections without fear of missing important information.

Turnkey Processing Facilities

UNIX facilities that support turnkey applications processing include the following:

- *System calls.* A set of over eighty system calls supports a variety of services and makes UNIX-based applications highly portable.

- *Process management.* The UNIX multiprocessing structure provides a tool for organizing applications.

- *File locking.* UNIX provides a mechanism for applications programs to synchronize concurrent update to a shared file.

- *Process scheduling.* UNIX uses scheduling algorithms that favor interactive, terminal-oriented tasks, keeping user response times low.

- *Memory management.* UNIX efficiently allocates main memory among concurrently executing tasks. Memory management techniques such as swapping and virtual memory permit effective interactive operation, even when memory is not large enough to hold all concurrently executing processes.

- *Pipes and interprocess communication.* The ability to pass data between processes allows sophisticated applications architectures to be built with the UNIX system.

- *Tailorable start-up procedures.* The UNIX start-up procedures can be customized to perform application-specific functions automatically.

- *Alternative user interfaces.* The UNIX system shell can be replaced with a user-developed program that provides an applications-oriented user interface to the UNIX system.

- *Terminal-independent applications.* Applications programs can use UNIX system facilities to insulate themselves from the particular characteristics of different brands of terminals that may be used on a UNIX system.

- *Shell scripts.* The shell forms an effective programming language for binding together applications programs into a total applications system. Shell scripts were discussed in Chapter 5.

UNIX System Calls

The UNIX system calls is the structure used by an application program to request services from the UNIX system kernel. System calls perform a variety of functions for applications programs. The calls are used, for example, to perform input and output, to create and remove files, to control processes, and to communicate between them. The set of approximately eighty system calls forms the interface between an application program and the UNIX system kernel.

Every UNIX system has exactly the same set of system calls, which perform exactly the same set of functions. The internals of the UNIX kernel may be radically different between a minicomputer UNIX system and a microprocessor-based UNIX system, but both systems will offer exactly the same set of system calls. The system call interface is a standard, which is unchanged from UNIX system to UNIX system.

This standardization makes applications software written for UNIX highly portable. An application program, such as a word processor, built on the system call interface, will execute on any UNIX system. No changes to the program's source code are required to move the program from one system to another. Applications developers can write their programs without having to worry about adapting them to run on different UNIX systems.

The standardization of the system call interface across a broad range of UNIX systems has resulted in a large and rapidly growing pool of high-quality software for the UNIX system. A software developer can be confident that its software will run on the large base of installed UNIX systems and on the new systems being introduced each month. Such is the power and impact of UNIX as an industry-standard operating system.

A detailed discussion of the system calls is beyond the scope of this text. They are of concern mainly to programmers, and even then, the system calls are usually used indirectly through the C language library routines. Appendix A lists the system calls, with a short description of each.

Process Management

The UNIX system's process management facilities allow applications programs to be efficiently structured. Foreground processes can interact with users, while background processes execute concurrently to handle non-interactive tasks. A process may start other processes to accomplish subtasks within an application. Interprocess communications facilities are also available to coordinate the work of the processes that comprise an application.

Recall that a process is a program in a state of execution. A process begins its life at the beginning of a program and lives as long as the program's instructions continue to specify new operations. When the program finally reaches a **halt**, **stop**, or **return** instruction (depending on the processor), the program terminates, and the process dies. Several UNIX system calls are available that alter the normal life cycle of a process.

The **exec** System Call

A single process may execute several different programs during its life by making use of the **exec** system call. Figure 7.1 shows what happens when a process makes this call. The kernel "transforms" the process into an execution of a new program. The kernel loads the new program into memory and resumes execution of the process at its beginning. The name of the new program is specified in the **exec** system call.

The new program begins execution with a considerable amount of history from its predecessor. Files opened by the previous program remain open for the new program. The process also retains its user-id and group-id.

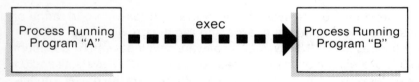

Fig. 7.1. *The EXEC System Call*

Figure 7.2 shows a simple example of how a sequence of report programs may be executed, using the **exec** call. The first program prints the first report before the program "execs" the second report program. The second program adds its report to the output file and execs the third report program, which finally closes the files and ends the process. The **exec** system call can be used much like the "program chaining" capability available in many other operating systems.

Fig. 7.2. *An EXEC Example*

The *fork* System Call

New processes are created in only one way: a currently active process requests creation of a new process through the **fork** system call. The new process that results is called the *child* process, and the original process is called the *parent* process. After the fork, both the parent and child processes are in execution. These processes are executing identical copies of the same program, with the same open files. Forking resembles the biological division of a cell into two identical cells.

Typically, the parent and child processes will not continue to execute the same program for very long. Immediately after the **fork** has been made, the child process will usually exec a new program. The result of the **fork/exec** combination is to create a new process that executes a new program. Both the parent and child processes are free to fork other processes, creating a hierarchy of processes with parent/child relationships.

The process hierarchy provides a natural way to structure menu-driven applications. Figure 7.3 shows a typical example, in which a **menu** program offers a choice of three data entry screens. When the user makes a selection, the **menu** program forks a child process, which execs the chosen program, and the data entry program runs to completion. Meanwhile, the **menu** program waits for completion of its child process, with a **wait** system call. Further execution of the **menu** program will resume when the data entry process dies. Figure 7.4 illustrates the **fork/exec** process for the menu application.

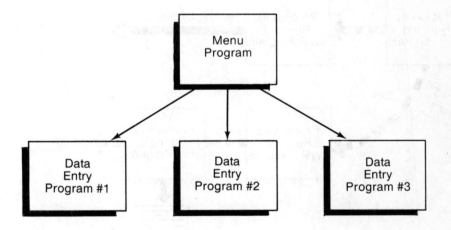

Fig. 7.3. *A Menu-Driven Application*

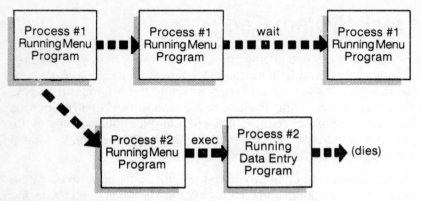

Fig. 7.4. *FORK and EXEC in a Menu-Driven Application*

In some applications, the parent process will not wait for the child process to die after a **fork**. For example, a word-processing program might print a document while allowing its user to continue editing another document. Figure 7.5 shows how this concurrent work can be accomplished. The **editor** program forks a child process, which execs the **printer** program to print the requested document. In this instance, the parent process continues to execute, allowing the user to edit other documents.

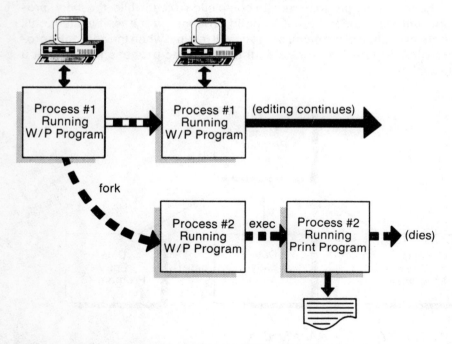

Fig. 7.5. *FORK and EXEC in a Word-Processing Application*

An Example: The Shell and Process Management

The shell uses the UNIX process structure to carry out user commands. Very few commands are built into the shell itself. In fact, most commands are separate utility programs, independent of the shell. When the shell process receives a command, the following operations take place:

1. The shell process forks a child process to execute the command.

2. The child process execs the utility program named in the command. Now two processes are running for the user—the shell (parent) process and the utility (child) process.

3. If the command is to be run in the foreground, the shell process waits for its child process to complete. The utility program may interact with the user at the terminal without interference from the shell. When the child process terminates, the shell prompts the user for the next command.

4. If the user requests background execution of the command, the shell process does not wait for the child process. Instead, the shell process prints the process-id of the child process and immediately prompts for the next command.

example

The shell's use of the process mechanism gives each user the ability to perform several different tasks on the system at once. Each request for background processing simply results in a new child process of the shell process.

The Environment of a Process

Each process on a UNIX system is launched with an *environment*, consisting of a set of named variables. The process may access these variables and obtain their values during its execution. These *environment variables* are the shell variables described in Chapter 5, whose values have been made part of the environment through the shell's **export** command. A process retains its environment across an **exec** system call; a child process inherits its parent's environment as a result of a **fork** system call.

Effective User-Id's

A process normally executes with the user-id of the user who initiates it. This user-id determines the process' permission to access files on the system and the process ability to make privileged system calls. A child process inherits its parent's user-id and, thus, the parent's permissions and privileges. Certain tasks, however, require that a process be able to execute with permissions and privileges that exceed those of its parent.

For example, suppose that payroll clerks will enter time-card data into a payroll file through a payroll data entry program. The payroll clerk should *not* have read access to the payroll file since it contains sensitive salary data. The data entry program, however, must have read access to the payroll file to verify correct data entry of employee numbers and other information. If the data entry program is executed simply on behalf of the data entry clerk, the program will not have the required read access permission.

UNIX solves this problem by allowing a process to execute with a user-id that is different from that of its parent. The process runs with an *effective user-id*, which is the user-id of the owner of the file containing the program, instead of the user-id of the parent process. Programs to be executed with an effective user-id are identified by a flag, which is stored with the ownership and permission information for the program file. This *set user-id* flag instructs the kernel to use an effective user-id when executing the program. A parallel *set group-id* flag causes the kernel to use an *effective group-id* when executing the program.

In the example, the payroll data entry program would be stored in a file whose owner had read access to the payroll file. The set user-id flag for the program would also be set. When the data entry clerk runs the program, it can successfully read the payroll file, even though the data entry clerk continues to be denied this access.

Extreme care must be taken to ensure that indiscriminate use of the effective user-id capability does not result in a breach of system security. Programs that set an effective user-id should be well debugged and severely limited in function.

File Sharing and Locking

The UNIX system allows a file to be accessed by many different programs at the same time. In an inventory control application, for example, several different programs may be reading data from an inventory master file, to retrieve price information in response to inventory part numbers typed by users.

A problem arises, however, if several programs attempt to share a file that will be updated or modified. For example, suppose two concurrent users are running a program that modifies quantity-on-hand data for parts in inventory. If both users attempt to modify the quantity-on-hand data for the same part at the same time, then the data in the file will not be updated correctly. Each user's program will first obtain the same quantity-on-hand data from the file, modify its value, and then place the modified data back into the file. However, only the second program to replace the data will have its change reflected in the file. The change made by the first program will simply be overwritten.

To permit correct concurrent update of files, UNIX includes system calls to synchronize concurrent file updates by multiple programs. These additional system calls implement a scheme known as *file locking*. Using the file-locking system calls, an application program can *lock* a particular range of bytes in a file, temporarily reserving them for its own exclusive use. The program can then retrieve data from that part of the file, modify it, and replace it in the file, with the assurance that no other program may access the data at the same time. The section of the file is released with another system call that *unlocks* it. If a second application program attempts to access part of a file that is locked by the first program, the UNIX kernel causes the second program to wait, with its execution suspended until the first program unlocks that part of the file.

The capability of the UNIX file-locking facility to lock any range of bytes in a file is powerful. By locking the entire range of bytes in a file, a program can obtain exclusive access to the file for bulk updates or other batch processing. By locking smaller byte ranges, the program can lock individual records in the file or even individual data items within a record.

UNIX actually provides two types of file locks:

- A *read lock* prevents any other program from reading or writing the locked region of the file. For example, if a program must update several pieces of data in a file and ensure that the data remains consistent to any other programs reading the file, the program can use a read lock. No other program can read the data items during the update, when they may be in an inconsistent state.

- A *write lock* prevents any other program from modifying the locked region of the file, but other programs may read data from the locked region. For example, if one program is updating data in a file but other programs may print reports based on the data during an update, the updating program can use a write lock. No other program can modify the data during the update, but other programs may read the data.

The choice of read or write locking is made at the time of the system call to lock the file.

UNIX also allows a file to be processed with either *mandatory* or *advisory* locking:

- *Mandatory locking* means that each system call that reads or writes data in the file is checked to make certain that the call does not violate a locked area of the file.

- *Advisory locking* means that file input/output system calls are not individually checked. Instead, only the calls to locked regions of the file are checked. The programmer has the responsibility to update data only within regions of the file that have been successfully locked.

The choice of mandatory or advisory locking is a tradeoff between data integrity and system efficiency. Although mandatory locking provides a greater guarantee of the integrity of data in a file, lock processing for each file input/output involves a fair amount of system overhead. Advisory locking eliminates this overhead and is generally safe for well-tested applications, but advisory locking leaves the possibility of undetected data corruption.

Another important feature of UNIX file locking is deadlock detection. When two programs are locking files, a condition called a *deadlock* can occur, as each program waits for the other to release its locks. For example, suppose that program A and program B are both processing an update for an employee's records. Program A has locked a personnel-file record, and program B has locked a payroll-file record. Now, each program tries to lock the employee's record in the other file. The result is a deadlock: program A waits for program B to release the payroll record while program B waits for program A to release the personnel record.

Happily, the UNIX kernel detects such deadlocks and automatically returns an error message to the program requesting the lock that would create a deadlock condition. This program's responsibility is to release its other locks and to try to process its update again at a later time.

Process Scheduling*

In a multiprocessing environment, with many processes competing for time on a single CPU, the system must continually decide which process to work on next. This decision is called *scheduling*, and it is one of the main functions of the UNIX system kernel. The kernel schedules processes for execution according to a priority scheme. Each active process has an associated priority; the kernel selects the highest-priority process for execution each time the CPU becomes available.

A process' priority fluctuates, depending on its recent behavior. UNIX discriminates in favor of processes that are I/O-intensive by gradually raising their priority. UNIX discriminates against processes that are CPU-intensive by gradually lowering their priority. Thus, UNIX favors I/O-intensive processes that only need the CPU for a short time. CPU-intensive processes "fill in" when there are no I/O-intensive processes ready to execute. This scheduling scheme results in good average response times for users performing interactive (I/O intensive) tasks, which is the typical environment for turnkey applications processing.

A process continues execution on the CPU until one of several events occurs. If the process performs an I/O operation or waits for some other system resource, the process will lose the CPU. A process will also lose the CPU after the process has executed for some fixed period of time (usually one second). This scheme prevents CPU-intensive processes from "hogging" the CPU, again ensuring good response times for interactive applications.

A user cannot improve the priority of his processes over other users' processes that are also executing on the system. Users can, however, *decrease* the priority of their processes with the **nice** utility. This utility is typically used for CPU-intensive background processes, such as the UNIX text-formatting utilities.

Memory Management*

Active processes take up main memory space on a UNIX system; their instructions and data must be loaded into main memory for execution. When only a few processes are active, they may all fit into main memory together. The CPU can switch between processes very rapidly, and system response time will be very good.

On a busy multiuser UNIX system, however, all the active processes cannot fit into main memory at once. UNIX handles this situation by keeping only some of the active processes in main memory and the rest on the disk. Active processes are then shuttled between memory and disk, as the CPU switches from process to process, giving each active process its turn for execution. The task of arranging the processes in main memory and moving them to and from the disk is called *memory management*, which is a function of the UNIX kernel.

The memory management scheme used by the kernel is closely tied to the computer's hardware. Some CPUs, for example, require that an entire process be stored in one contiguous location in main memory. Other CPUs allow a process to be broken into pieces and scattered all over memory. Some CPUs require that an entire process be loaded into memory before it can be executed. Others allow a process to execute with only a few pieces of the process in memory. The memory management function in the kernel must therefore be customized for each new computer system to which UNIX is ported.

Two major memory management techniques are used in current versions of the UNIX system. The first, called *swapping*, is the traditional UNIX memory management scheme. The second, called *virtual memory*, was first used in the Berkeley versions of the UNIX system and is now the standard scheme for UNIX System V. Both of these memory management schemes are described in detail in the following sections.

*Process Swapping**

Swapping is the UNIX memory management technique used on systems that require an entire process to be present in main memory for execution. The technique is used in the AT&T versions of the UNIX system, as well as in most of the current minicomputer and microcomputer versions.

Swapping shuttles entire processes between the memory and a reserved area of the disk, known as the *swap area*. When a process in main memory has received its share of the CPU's available time, the process is *swapped out* (copied to the swap area), and one or more of the active processes on the disk are *swapped in* (copied into main memory) so that the CPU can work on them.

Swapping diminishes the performance of the system, as perceived by each user. When swapping, the system must spend a small percentage of its time shuttling processes between disk and memory, which reduces the time available for actual process execution. But the overhead of swapping is ordinarily worth this inconvenience, since swapping allows a UNIX system to run more processes than could otherwise fit into main memory at one time. The alternative is not to allow some of the processes to execute at all!

If the system attempts to work on many more processes than can fit into main memory at once, swapping can become a heavy burden. When the system spends a high percentage of its time on swapping, response time for interactive users will increase dramatically. (This phenomenon is known as *thrashing.*) There are two alternatives to remedy this problem: reduce the load on the system by moving some users to other machines or purchase more memory so that more processes can fit into main memory at one time.

To maximize swapping's efficiency, the kernel uses a dedicated area on the disk for this technique. A copy of each process is made in this swap area when the process is first started, and the copy is updated each time the process is swapped out. The process image is removed from the swap area when the process dies, making room for the swapping of other processes. Even if the program is requested again a few seconds later, a fresh copy of it must be created in the swap area.

*The Sticky Bit**

On a typical UNIX system, a handful of utility programs account for the vast majority of the commands executed by users. Constantly reloading these programs into the swap area for execution becomes a drain on system performance, especially if the programs are large. The system administrator can instruct UNIX to keep permanent copies of these frequently executed programs in the swap area. This instruction is given by setting the program file's *sticky bit*, a flag stored with the ownership and access permissions for the file.

When a program's sticky bit is set, its process image remains permanently in the swap area, even after the process dies. On subsequent executions, the program can be loaded very quickly, since the process image is already in the swap area. In a system used for program development, likely candidates for the sticky bit are the shell, the editor, and the C compiler. In a turnkey system, the most heavily used data entry and inquiry programs are candidates for the sticky bit.

Virtual Memory*

Many newer computer systems feature memory management hardware that does not require an entire process to be loaded into memory in order to execute it. Instead, the CPU can execute a process with only a part of the process that is not loaded, the hardware detects this condition, and the operating system brings the missing part into memory. The technique of breaking an active process into pieces, which are brought into main memory only as they are needed, is called *virtual memory*.

Virtual memory hardware is available on most superminicomputers and mainframes. It is also available on the new generation of advanced microprocessors, such as the Motorola M68010, the Intel iAPX 386, and the National Semiconductor 16032. The Berkeley versions of the UNIX system have pioneered software support for virtual memory operation. Virtual memory, now available with AT&T UNIX systems, will become widely used as more systems are based on new microprocessors.

Virtual memory has two major benefits. It allows a UNIX system to execute very large programs, even those that are many times larger than the available main memory on the system. Virtual memory can also be more efficient than swapping, since portions of a greater number of processes can be retained in main memory at the same time.

Shared Libraries

The latest versions of UNIX include an advanced feature, called *shared libraries*, that can significantly improve the performance of UNIX memory management. Figure 7.6 illustrates how shared libraries work and contrasts them with ordinary libraries.

A significant part of a typical program's code is comprised of *library routines*—prewritten routines that provide commonly used functions, such as input/output and mathematical computation. For small programs, as much as 50 percent of the program's size may be attributable to these library routines. Ordinarily, each program has its own private copy of the library routines it uses. These routines are bound into the program as part of the program-development process. As shown in the figure, when several programs are running concurrently, the duplication of library routines in each program can lead to a substantial waste of memory.

With a shared library, the UNIX system does not bind a copy of the library routines into an application program. Instead, the executable program includes *pointers* to the library routines. When the program begins to execute,

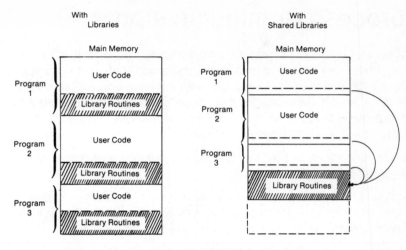

Fig. 7.6. *Saving Memory by Using Shared Libraries*

UNIX automatically fills in these pointers, linking the application to a copy of the library routines already in main memory. Thus, a single copy of the library routines can be shared by all concurrently executing programs.

Shared libraries provide three advantages for a UNIX system:

- They conserve main memory. The shared libraries are stored in main memory only once instead of duplicated library routines in every executing program.

- They conserve disk space. The library routines are not bound into each executable program, so the size of executable programs stored on the disk is smaller.

- They allow transparent library updates. Improvements and bug fixes in the library routines are used automatically by executing programs as soon as the changes are installed in the shared library. Without shared libraries, application programs must be relinked to take advantage of these improvements.

UNIX System V provides a shared version of the standard C library. In addition, applications designers can use the **mkshrlib** (**make shared lib**rary) utility to add their own commonly used routines to the shared library and further improve the efficiency of system operation.

Interprocess Communications*

Many applications are most conveniently implemented as a family of cooperating processes. For example, a data base inquiry application may be built with a "front-end" process that interacts with the user and a "back-end server" process, which accesses the data base. Such applications rely on the kernel to provide process-to-process communications services that tie the individual processes into a single application.

UNIX offers several tools for process-to-process communications, including the following:

- A *pipe* is the oldest and most widely used tool for communicating between processes. It provides a one-way data path for a stream of data between a sending process and a receiving process.

- A *named pipe* is a more permanent form of a pipe, which is identified by a name, just like a UNIX file or device. A named pipe can be used for communication between two unrelated processes.

- The *IPC message facility* allows two processes to communicate by sending messages through a message queue in main memory. Unlike a pipe, message queues operate on discrete "messages" instead of byte streams, and a single message queue can support multiple senders and multiple receivers of data.

- *Shared memory* allows two processes to share access to a portion of the system's main memory, allowing bi-directional communication between the processes as fast as they can modify memory contents.

- *Semaphores* are data structures used to control the sharing of a serially shareable resource (such as a line printer or shared memory) between processes. By using a semaphore, the processes can synchronize their use of the resource and prevent errors.

Each of these interprocess communication techniques is described in more detail in the following sections.

*Pipes**

Recall from Chapter 5 that the shell uses pipes to connect programs in a sequence, sending the standard output of one program to the standard input of the next. Actually, pipes are not a feature of the shell, but rather a service provided by the kernel. Pipes can be used by applications programs to send messages from one process to another.

A pipe is a one-way communication path between processes. The *sending* process puts messages into the pipe, and the *receiving* process removes them. The pipe is perceived by each process to be an ordinary file. If two-way communication is required, two pipes are used, one for message traffic in each direction.

The kernel manages a pipe on a first-in-first-out basis. The sending process places data into the pipe with the standard **write** system call. The kernel holds the data until the receiving process requests the data with the standard **read** system call. Data is supplied to the receiving process in exactly the same order in which the data was placed into the pipe by the sending process. Figure 7.7 shows two processes connected by a pipe.

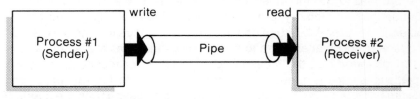

Fig. 7.7. *The UNIX Pipe Feature*

Typically, the processes connected by a pipe will send and receive data at different rates. The kernel automatically synchronizes the sending and receiving processes, forcing the sending process to wait if the pipe becomes full, and forcing the receiving process to wait if the pipe becomes empty. Synchronization is completely transparent to the programs themselves.

Named Pipes*

Pipes are limited by the requirement that both the sending and receiving process have a common parent process. This limitation is imposed because the pipe is a temporary structure, created by a process and destroyed when the process dies. Both ends of the pipe are created when the pipe comes into being, and thus both ends must be used by descendants of the process that creates the pipe.

Named pipes are a newer form of pipe, which address this limitation. Unlike the temporary pipe created by a process, a named pipe has a more permanent form. By convention, named pipes are placed in the **/dev** directory and appear as special files, just like the "real" devices in that directory. An application program can establish access to the named pipe just as the program establishes access to a file by opening the pipe by name to write data into or read data from the pipe.

Except for its more permanent nature, a named pipe operates just like a normal pipe. The named pipe provides a tool for synchronized one-way transmission of a byte stream between a sending process and receiving process.

The IPC Message Facility*

The IPC Message Facility provides an alternative to pipes for sending messages between cooperating processes. Unlike a pipe, however, which passes a continuous stream of data, the IPC message facility deals in discrete messages. Figure 7.8 shows how the facility works.

The first process to use the message facility requests allocation of a message queue in main memory to handle the passage of messages between processes. Other processes then can use the same queue to send or receive messages. A process attempting to send a message uses a system call to place the message into the message queue. Other processes also may place messages into the queue, which maintains a first-in-first-out order for the messages. When a process attempts to read a message from the queue, the process uses a system call and is given the first available message. Just as the message queue supports multiple senders, multiple processes can request messages from the queue. UNIX optionally provides synchronization to block execution of a process that tries to read a message from the queue when no messages are available.

The message queue provides an effective way to implement an application where several "requester" processes are requesting services and several "server" processes are providing the services. An example of such an application is line printer spooling when more than one printer can provide printing services.

Shared Memory and Semaphores*

The shared memory feature allows a portion of system memory to be dedicated for sharing among multiple processes. Processes access shared memory with UNIX system calls, opening the memory area by name to read and write data stored there. Data placed in the shared memory area by one process is immediately accessible to all other processes. The processes are thus closely coupled, and interprocess communication is very fast. Figure 7.8 illustrates shared memory operation.

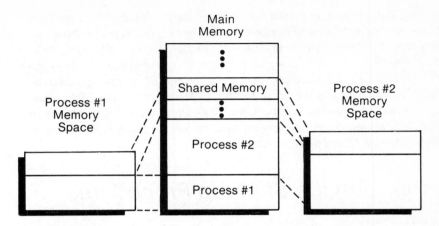

Fig. 7.8. *Shared Memory Operation*

Each process using a shared memory region sees the memory area as if it were a part of the process's own local program. When one process changes the value of a program variable stored in the shared memory, the change is immediately visible to all the other cooperating processes because the values of their variables also change. If two processes are modifying the same data item in shared memory, they must carefully coordinate their updates to prevent data-integrity problems. The IPC Semaphore facility is often used to provide this coordination.

Processes can use semaphores to coordinate access to shared memory. Before modifying data in the shared memory, a process will use a semaphore to lock out access by other processes. Other processes using the semaphore will be forced to wait if they attempt to access the shared memory while it is still locked by the first process. Semaphores are used through a set of UNIX system calls.

A discussion of the additional capabilities of semaphores and shared memory is beyond the scope of this text. These features offer applications designers powerful tools for building complex, tightly coupled, multiprocessing applications.

Building a Turnkey Application

UNIX provides applications designers with a modular system structure that can be easily customized to meet specific applications requirements. The UNIX start-up procedures can be tailored to place the system automatically into an applications processing mode without user intervention. The login procedure can be modified to perform application-specific processing before admitting a user to the system. The standard UNIX shell can be replaced with an alternative user interface that prompts and guides the user through application choices. Applications can be insulated from terminal dependencies. Finally, programs can be automatically executed at specified times without manual intervention. In short, the UNIX system can be transformed into a turnkey applications processing system, whose users have no need to understand UNIX concepts or commands.

Customizing the Start-Up Procedures

The standard UNIX start-up procedure executes a sequence of four UNIX utilities to create a multiuser environment. Immediately after the system is booted, the kernel launches the **init** utility, which initializes the system and prepares it to accept user logins. The **getty** utility displays the login prompt on a terminal screen and accepts the user name. The **login** utility validates the user name and password and starts the shell to accept commands from the user. When a user logs out, the shell process terminates, and the **init** process is responsible for starting the login procedure all over again. Figure 7.9 illustrates the start-up sequence and the relationships among the utility programs that comprise it.

The **init** utility switches the UNIX system between various modes of operation, called *init states*. Most UNIX systems support at least two init states: single-user (used for system maintenance) and multiuser (used for daily processing). On networked systems, an additional init state is usually defined to support multiuser operation with Remote File Sharing active. An application designer can define additional init states to meet specific requirements. For example, an application may require a "normal hours" operating mode in which all the terminals are active, an "off hours" mode in which only a few terminals are active, and a "maintenance" mode in which only the system console is active.

The **init** utility is completely table-driven, taking its instructions from an initialization file named **/etc/inittab**. An application designer can modify this table to specify the application-specific processing that is to occur during the start-up procedures. The initialization file normally causes the file **/etc/rc** to be executed as a shell script. This script usually performs file system checks, purges temporary files, starts system accounting, and so on. The script may also be modified to customize the start-up sequence. Typically, a separate **/etc/rc** file for each init state specifies the processing to be performed when the system enters that state.

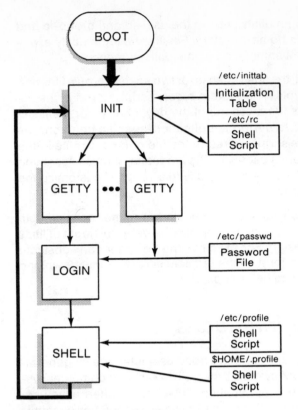

Fig.7.9. *UNIX Start-Up Sequence*

In standard multiuser operation, **init** spawns one child process per terminal. Each of these child processes executes the **getty** utility, which displays the login prompt, accepts the user's name, and executes the **login** utility. The **login** utility verifies the user name and password against the list of authorized users stored in the **/etc/passwd** file. This file contains one entry per user. Each entry includes the following critical pieces of information:

- The user name
- The encrypted password
- The user-id
- The group-id to be used on login
- The real name of the user
- The name of the home directory
- The name of the program to be launched after successful login (usually the shell)

If login is successful, the **login** utility sets up the user-id and group-id and places the user in the user's home directory. Finally, the **login** utility execs the shell, marking successful completion of the login sequence.

Before displaying its prompt, the shell checks for two special *profile* files and executes them as shell scripts. The *system profile* script, stored in the file **/etc/profile**, typically prints the message of the day, checks for mail, etc. This script can be modified to perform application-specific functions, as necessary. The *user profile* script, stored in the file named **.profile** in the user's home directory, performs user-specific functions, such as assigning values to shell variables. The user can modify this script to customize the user's own start-up sequence.

If an application requires special security checking or other special login processing, the application designer can replace the **getty** and **login** utilities with programs of special design. For example, the designer can substitute programs that display a login form on the terminal screen or that download code into an intelligent terminal before operation.

Alternative User Interfaces

The standard UNIX system shell provides a good user interface for general-purpose processing on a UNIX system. When a UNIX-based computer system is dedicated to a particular application, however, an alternative user interface may be better suited to the needs of system users. For example, many programmers prefer the *C-shell*, an alternative shell from the Berkeley UNIX version with special features that support software development. For turnkey applications processing, menu shells offer a simple method of providing a limited set of application choices to the user.

UNIX makes it simple for applications designers to replace the standard UNIX shell with an alternative user interface. For each user, the name of the program that is to be launched, following a successful login, is stored in the **/etc/passwd** file. Normally, this program is the standard UNIX shell. However, an alternative program may be specified simply by replacing the name of the shell, **/bin/sh**, with another program name.

Terminal-Independent Applications

A UNIX system may have many different kinds of terminals connected to it, each with different hardware and software characteristics. The **stty** utility is used to configure the UNIX system for operation with different types of terminals and communications protocols. The **curses/terminfo** facility is a set of routines and files that supports the development of applications programs which are independent of variations in terminal characteristics. This facility replaces a similar capability, called the **termcap** facility, that was available on earlier UNIX versions.

The **stty** utility informs the kernel of terminal and communications line characteristics. This utility is used to specify the data communications speed of the terminal (for example, 2,400 or 9,600 baud); whether parity checking will be performed; characters for backspacing and end-of-file; and similar characteristics. The kernel adapts to these characteristics, insulating applications programs from them.

In addition, screen-oriented applications programs need to perform control operations on a terminal, such as clearing the screen or moving the cursor to a particular position on the screen. The control codes that perform these functions vary from terminal to terminal. The **curses/terminfo** facility helps to insulate applications programs from these variations. The **terminfo** database contains information about the capabilities and control codes for commonly used terminals. Each entry in the database corresponds to a particular brand of terminal, identified by a name. Terminal descriptions are prepared using a UNIX editor and then compiled using the terminfo compiler utility, **tic**. The compiled descriptions are stored in the **terminfo** database.

For each user logged onto the system, the environment variable **TERM** is set to one of the terminal names in the **terminfo** database; the name identifies the terminal brand for that user. An application program can obtain the value of **TERM** and query the **terminfo** database to obtain information about that terminal's characteristics. The application program then can adjust its output to include the control sequences that are appropriate to that terminal brand.

The **terminfo** database is also used by the **curses** facility. **Curses** is a set of terminal input/output routines originally developed as part of the Berkeley UNIX system. The objective of **curses** is to insulate the application program from the terminal's characteristics. Instead of sending information directly to the terminal screen, a program using **curses** calls various **curses** routines to position the cursor, clear the screen, transmit characters, and receive input. **Curses** uses the information in the **terminfo** database to carry out the requested operation.

The **curses** facility also provides optimization of screen output, as shown in Figure 7.10. **Curses** does not send each request for terminal output directly to the terminal screen. Instead, **curses** keeps track of the current appearance of the screen and accumulates the program's changes on an internal "virtual screen," which the **curses** facility maintains in memory. When the application program has finished a series of output operations, the program explicitly asks **curses** to update the screen. The **curses** facility then determines, for the specific terminal being used, the optimal sequence of output operations to apply the changes to the current screen. In this way, the application program can be written to update sections of the screen at will, leaving concerns about input/output efficiency to **curses**.

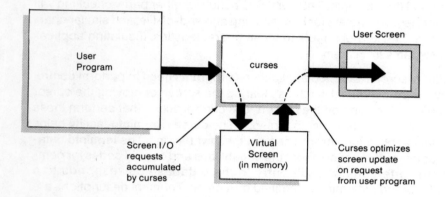

Fig. 7.10. *Using the Curses Facility To Optimize Screen Output*

Curses also supports advanced terminal features in a terminal-independent way, including the following:

- Display attributes such as blinking and underline
- Softkeys or other function key labels
- Variations in screen size
- Line drawing character sets
- Windowing, the capability to interact with subareas of the screen as if they were independent terminals

Automatic Program Execution

Turnkey applications often include functions that must be performed repeatedly on a periodic basis. System backup, for example, may be performed each evening during nonworking hours, to ensure easy recovery from any errors that may occur. Or an application may transmit a transaction file to a mainframe for processing twice a day, at regularly scheduled hours.

The UNIX utility **cron** can be used to perform automatically these periodic functions, without manual intervention by the system administrator or other users. A table stored in the file **/etc/crontab** lists the programs to be periodically executed and the specific times when they are to be run. The **cron** utility reads this file and causes the programs to be executed as requested. Normally, the utility is started as a background process by the UNIX system start-up sequence and executes continuously. The system administrator is responsible for maintaining the **/etc/crontab** file.

CHAPTER
8

File Processing

O f over three hundred UNIX system utilities, a large number—perhaps the majority—are used to process text or data in files. These file-processing utilities offer the user a wide range of functions. Some utilities are particularly useful on text files; others are designed to work on tabular data in the familiar row-column format. In typical UNIX style, each utility is specialized and designed to do one thing well. Taken as a group, the utilities give the user a powerful array of tools to manipulate file contents.

Many file-processing utilities are filters, each of which takes a single input file and processes its contents into a single output file. This action makes filters even more useful when they are combined in pipelines. A sequence of simple utilities can perform complex file-processing operations, eliminating the need to develop custom file-processing programs.

This chapter describes the general-purpose file-processing utilities. Those that have a more specialized use (for example, typesetting or program debugging) are described in the following chapters.

The following functions are available through the file-processing utilities:

- Splitting and combining files
- Comparing file contents
- Searching and modifying file contents
- Sorting and ordering file contents
- Manipulating tabular data
- Compressing and encrypting files

135

> *Note:* The command descriptions in this chapter include examples based on a **results** file whose contents are described in Figure 8.1. The **results** file contains lines that represent individual sales orders. Each line consists of five fields that list, in order, the salesperson, the office, the region, the customer number, and the amount of the sale.

The results file contains a five-column table:

Jones	boston	east	0221349	60000
Jones	boston	east	0213412	57995
Davis	boston	east	0210497	4650
Harris	newyork	east	0491207	19425
Harris	newyork	east	0421007	30000
Andrews	phila	east	0412095	2950
salesperson	office	region	customer number	amount

Fig. 8.1. *Contents of Results File*

Combining and Splitting Files

Many applications require that information in different files be combined together or that a single large file be split into several smaller ones. For example, data from several different laboratory experiments may be stored in separate files, which must be combined for analysis. Chapters of a manuscript may be stored in different files, which must be combined to form a complete text. In another application, accounting transactions may be kept in a single large file, which must be split into smaller files for department-by-department expense reporting. In each of these examples, standard UNIX utilities can perform the file processing. Table 8.1 lists the utilities that split and combine files.

Combining Files with cat

Perhaps the most frequently used file-processing utility is **cat** (con**cat**enate files), which combines the contents of several files into a single file. The files to be combined are named in sequence on the command line:

```
$ cat boston/results newyork/results
   .
   .
   .
```

Table 8.1
Utilities that Split and Combine Files

head	Copies text from the beginning of a file to the standard output
tail	Copies text from the end of a file to the standard output
split	Divides a large file into a sequence of smaller files
csplit	Divides a file into sections (like **split**), but splits based on patterns in the file
cat	Combines the contents of several files into one large file
scat	Operates like **cat**, but breaks lines longer than 79 characters into multiple lines, for ease of reading on terminals and 80-column printers

The **cat** utility copies the contents of the first file to the standard output, followed by contents of the second file, and so on, until all the files have been copied. This process is illustrated in Figure 8.2. If there is only one file in the list, the **cat** utility simply copies the contents of the file to the standard output. This copying is often done in order to list a file's contents on a terminal. The command

```
$ cat boston/results newyork/results phila/results>results
   .
   .
   .
```

is used in conjunction with output redirection, to store the contents of several files in a single output file.

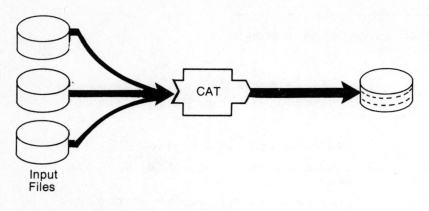

Input
Files

Fig. 8.2. *Concatenating Files with CAT*

Splitting Files with **split** *and* **csplit**

The **split** and **csplit** utilities are the opposite of **cat**. They take a single large file and divide it into several smaller ones. Figure 8.3 illustrates the operation of these utilities. The **split** utility divides a file into files with equal numbers of lines, regardless of the file's contents. This utility can be used, for example, to divide a file of 10,000 lines into ten files of 1,000 lines each, which can then be more easily edited.

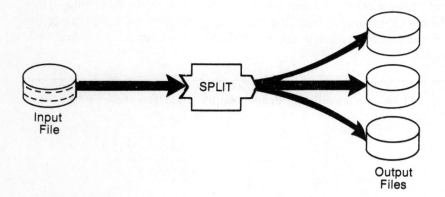

Input
File

Output
Files

Fig. 8.3. *Splitting Files with SPLIT*

The **csplit** utility gives the user more control over how the file is split. A series of *patterns*, given on the command line, is matched against the lines in the input file. The **csplit** utility copies lines from the input file into an output file and starts a new output file each time the next pattern specified on the command line is matched. For example, the **results** file in Figure 8.1 contains sales results for all the eastern region sales offices, sorted in order by office. Each line of the file contains the name of the office from which the sale was made. The command

```
$ csplit results /newyork/ /phila/
18Ø
12Ø
6Ø
$ ∎
```

creates a separate output file containing the results for each sales office and prints out the number of bytes contained in each output file. More complex splits are also possible.

Other utilities in this group include **head** and **tail**, which select only the beginning or end of a file for processing, and **scat**, a variation of the **cat** utility.

Comparing and Contrasting Files

It is often useful to compare the contents of two files to see if they are the same, or if they are not, to determine the nature of their differences. For example, a user may make a copy of a critical file and then want to compare it to the original to be certain that the copy was made correctly. Or a user may have two files, one containing quarter-to-date sales transactions and the other containing month-to-date transactions. The user may want to obtain the differences in the two files, to get a list of transactions up to, but not including, the current month. In another example, a user who has been interrupted while editing a file may have forgotten exactly which changes were made. Comparing the "before editing" file with the "after editing" file gives a quick list of the changes. Standard UNIX utilities can be used for these and other file comparison functions. Table 8.2 lists some of these utilities.

Comparing Files

A simple utility for comparing files is **cmp** (**comp**are). Given the names of two files, this utility compares them and prints the position in the two files where they first differ. For example, the command

```
$ cmp results1 results2
results1 results2 differ: char 28, line 2
$ ▪
```

Table 8.2
File Comparison Utilities

cmp	Compares two files, either reporting that they are identical or giving the position where they first differ
comm	Compares two sorted files, reporting on lines that are common to both, lines that appear only in the first file, and lines that appear only in the second file
sdiff	Compares two files, generating a side-by-side listing of their contents
diff	Compares two files and generates a list of the actions that are required to edit the first file so that it is identical to the second file
diff3	Compares three files and generates a list of their differences
dircmp	Compares three files and generates various tabulated information about their contents
sum	Computes a checksum based on the contents of a file
wc	Counts the number of lines, words, and characters in a file

indicates that the two files first differ at the twenty-eighth character position, which occurs on the second line of the file. If the files are identical, then **cmp** prints nothing. Figure 8.4 illustrates the operation of **cmp**.

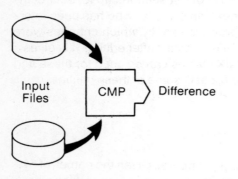

Fig. 8.4. *Comparing Files with CMP*

More information on file differences is provided by the **comm** and **sdiff** utilities. The **comm** utility takes two sorted files, compares them, and generates a three-column output report. The first column lists lines that appear only in the first file, the second column lists lines that appear only in the second file, and the third column lists lines that appear in both files. The **sdiff** utility produces an alternative two-column report, where lines from the two files are listed side by side. A one-character column between the side-by-side listings labels each line as unique to one file, unique to the other, or identical in both files.

Contrasting Files

Often users will want to compare two versions of the same file, one of which is an edited version of the other. The **diff** utility, as well as several others, is used for this kind of comparison. The output of the **diff** utility is a list of editing actions; when allied to the contents of the first file, these actions will generate the second, edited file. Editing actions include adding a line, deleting a line, or changing a line.

An option to the **diff** command causes output to be generated in the form of actual commands for the UNIX text editor (described in Chapter 9). With this option, the user can store only an original file, plus a short sequence of editor commands produced by the **diff** utility. These commands can be applied to the original file to recreate a later version of the file whenever it is needed. If the files are large and the differences between them are minor, this method can be very efficient in storing different versions of the same file on a UNIX system.

Word Counts and Checksums

A simple utility named **wc** (**w**ord **c**ount) counts and prints the number of lines, words, and characters in a file. If the file contains a list of items, such as a list of sales personnel, the **wc** utility offers an easy way to count the number of items in the list. This utility is frequently used in pipelines to count the number of items produced by the preceding command. For example, the pipeline

```
$ ls | wc -l
12
$ ■
```

counts the number of files in the current directory, by counting the lines in the output of the **ls** command. (The option **-l** instructs **wc** to count lines only.) The **wc** utility is yet another method for determining that two files are not identical, by discovering that they do not contain the same number of lines, words, or characters.

Another utility, named **sum** (check**sum**), calculates and prints a checksum on the contents of a file. A *checksum* is a number that results from arithmetically adding the contents of each computer word in the file. Two identical files will have the same checksum. It is unlikely that two nonidentical files will have the same checksum. Thus, two files with the same checksum have a high probability of being identical.

Searching and Modifying File Contents

A common file-processing operation is searching the contents of a file for a particular piece of information. For example, a sales manager may want to search the forecast file for all orders forecasted by a particular salesperson, to focus special attention on that person. In another application, an accounts receivable file may be searched, listing out all accounts with outstanding balances older than sixty days. Or perhaps a set of files containing the text of several contracts must be searched for a particular clause or phrase.

Standard UNIX file-processing utilities can easily perform these kinds of searching and modifying tasks. File-searching utilities offer some of the most complex processing functions of all the file-processing utilities. These utilities can search a file for lines that match one or more patterns and then undertake a complex series of actions when matching lines are found in the file. Despite their ability to handle complex operations, file-searching utilities are most often used in fairly simple ways, as illustrated in the examples that follow. Table 8.3 summarizes the file-searching and modification utilities.

File Searching with **grep**

The **grep** (**g**lobal **r**egular **e**xpression **p**rint) utility is the standard file-searching and selection utility. Figure 8.5 shows how it operates. The user specifies a pattern to guide **grep**'s search through a file. This utility examines the input file, line by line, checking each one to see if it contains the pattern.

Table 8.3
File-Searching and Modification Utilities

file	Makes intelligent guesses as to the contents of a file
grep	Searches an input file for lines that match a pattern and copies them to the standard output file
sed	Applies a set of user-specified editing commands to one or more input files
awk	Searches an input file for lines that match one of a set of patterns and performs a user-specified action for each pattern matched
dd	Performs common transformations on one or more input files, to produce an output file
tr	Passes through a file, character by character, selectively replacing or deleting characters
newform	Reformats lines of a text file according to user specifications

When a match is found, the line is copied to the standard output file. If a line does not contain the pattern, the line is not copied to the output file. When **grep** has completed its search, the output file contains the input file's lines that contain the pattern.

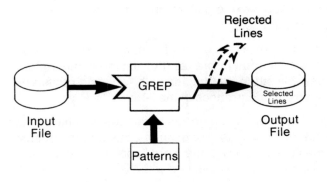

Fig. 8.5. *Searching Files with GREP*

For example, to search the file **results** for sales from the Boston sales office, the user would type the following command:

```
$ grep boston results
Jones     boston     east      0221349    60000
Jones     boston     east      0213412    57995
Davis     boston     east      0210497     4650
$ ∎
```

The **grep** utility copies to the standard output only the lines that contain the word "boston" somewhere in each line.

The **grep** utility also acts as a filter in a pipeline. When used in a pipeline, **grep** selects some of the output of the preceding program for subsequent processing by the next program in the pipeline.

The patterns used by the **grep** utility are called *regular expressions* (hence, the strange name of the command). The flexible pattern-matching features of **grep** provide the following capabilities:

- Match any single character in a particular position, by including the wild-card character *dot* (**.**)

- Match a specific set of characters in a particular position, by enclosing the characters in *square brackets* (for example, **[abc]**)

- Match zero or more occurrences of a character, by following it with an *asterisk* (∗) (For example, the pattern **abc**∗ matches the strings "ab", "abccc", "abcccccc", etc.)

- Match a bounded range of occurrences of a character, by enclosing the upper and lower bounds in *braces* (For example, the pattern **abc{4,7}** matches any string that begins with "ab" and continues with from four to seven occurrences of the letter "c.")

- Match the beginning or end of a line, using the special characters *circumflex* (^) and *dollar sign* ($) (For example, the pattern **^boston** only matches lines that begin with the word "boston," and the pattern **boston$** only matches lines that end with the word.)

Options to the **grep** utility permit the user to select lines that do *not* match the pattern, to output only the line numbers of the lines that match, and so on. The **grep** utility can also read its patterns from a file rather than from the command line. This feature is useful for handling complex patterns.

More Complex Pattern Matching with *awk*

The **grep** utility provides sophisticated pattern-matching capability, but a limited choice of actions for lines that match the patterns. Each line of the input file is either placed or not placed in the output file; no further processing of the line is performed. The **awk** utility extends pattern-matching processing much further. This utility, therefore, can be used as a sophisticated report-writing tool.

Like **grep**, the **awk** utility passes through a file, line by line, attempting to match each line to a set of patterns. But for each pattern, **awk** allows the user to specify what *action* is to be taken when a line that matches the pattern is encountered. The user may instruct the **awk** utility to scan through the **results** file, searching for lines that contain sales from the eastern region, printing column headers, accumulating total orders, and adding the cumulative total to the end of each line as it is sent to the output file.

Figure 8.6 shows how the **awk** utility operates. The patterns that control **awk**'s operation can be specified on the command line, or they can be stored in a file. For each pattern, the user also specifies a corresponding action.

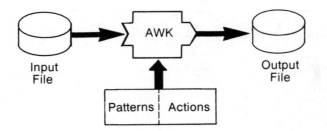

Fig. 8.6. *Pattern Matching with AWK*

The **awk** utility considers each line in the input file to be made up of one or more *fields*, which are separated by one or more blanks. Each field can be individually referenced, both in the patterns and in the actions. The patterns used by **awk** are like those described for the **grep** utility in the preceding section. The actions taken form the basis of a comprehensive report-writing language with the following capabilities:

- Variable assignment and arithmetic computation
- Copying fields from the input line to the output file

- Sending formatted output to the output file

- Conditional testing (**if** . . . **then** . . . **else**)

- Looping (**while** . . . **do**)

- Iteration (**for** . . . **next**)

A detailed description of **awk**'s processing capabilities is beyond the scope of this text. The utility's notation is cryptic and difficult for a novice to understand. Yet the amount of processing that can be expressed with just a few lines is amazing. A C language program that performs the same processing might contain over a hundred lines of source code. A COBOL or Pascal program would be at least that long. In the hands of an experienced user, **awk** is a powerful and efficient report-generating tool that reduces the need for developing new file-processing programs.

File Editing with *sed*

Another pattern-matching utility with powerful processing capabilities is **sed** (stream **ed**itor). The **sed** utility is an "automatic" version of the UNIX text editor **ed**, described in Chapter 9. Figure 8.7 illustrates **sed**'s operation.

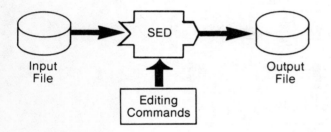

Fig. 8.7. *Editing Files with SED*

The **sed** utility reads lines, one by one, from an input file and applies a set of editing commands to the lines. The edited lines are then sent to the standard output file. The **sed** editing commands take exactly the same form as commands to the **ed** utility. However, **sed** operates on only a single line at a time and can be used to edit files that are too large for the **ed** text editor.

The editing commands used with **sed** include a pattern-matching capability like the one offered by **grep** and **awk**. But the **sed** editing commands offer more flexibility in adding, deleting, modifying, and searching lines of the input file as it is processed. In addition, **sed** can copy lines from the input file into a "holding buffer" and copy them to new positions in the output file. This utility can also merge lines from other files into the output file. The **sed** editing commands may be specified on the command line or stored in a file.

File Sorting Utilities

Often the contents of a file must be sorted into some order before useful processing can proceed. The **sort** utility performs this function. The utility takes lines from one or more input files and sorts them, producing a standard output file containing the lines in sorted order. With **sort**, each line from an input file is treated as a series of one or more fields, separated from one another by spaces. The **sort** utility can reorder the file based on one or more of the fields.

For example, the **results** file may be sorted in order by the amount of each sale, for sales analysis. The command

```
$ sort +4nr results
Jones    boston    east    0221349    60000
Jones    boston    east    0213412    57995
Harris   newyork   east    0421007    30000
Harris   newyork   east    0491207    19425
Davis    boston    east    0210497     4650
Andrews  phila     east    0412095     2950
$ ■
```

will do the job. The **+4** on the command line instructs **sort** to skip the first four fields and sort on the fifth (amount) field. The **n** identifies the field as numeric, and the **r** instructs **sort** to reverse the sorting order so that the sales with the largest amounts appear first.

Additional options to the **sort** utility instruct it to sort based on multiple fields, merge multiple files, and perform other sophisticated processing. Other utilities are available to perform further sorting and ordering functions, as shown in Table 8.4.

Table 8.4
File-Sorting and Ordering Utilities

sort	Sorts the lines of one or more files into order, using one or more sort keys
uniq	Finds and eliminates duplicate lines in a file, and is often used with **sort**
nl	Produces an output file by inserting the line number of each line of an input file at the beginning of each line
tsort	Accepts as input a partial ordering and produces a fully ordered list of the items

Processing Tabular Data

It is often useful to organize information in a file as a *table*, with the data neatly arranged into rows and columns. Each *row* of the table is stored as one line in the file. Each *column* in a row is stored as one field in the line, separated from adjacent columns by one or more spaces. The **results** file is an example of such a table. Several utilities described earlier in this chapter are useful with tabular files. For example, the **sort** utility is convenient for sorting the rows of a table into order, based on the contents of one or more columns. The **grep** utility is also useful in selecting only certain rows of a table, for further processing, as illustrated in Figure 8.8. Table 8.5 lists several additional utilities that are uniquely well suited for row-column processing on tabular files.

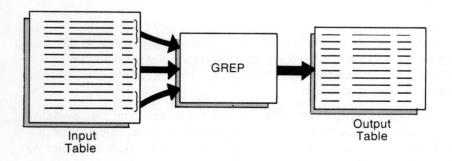

Input Table

GREP

Output Table

Fig. 8.8. *Selecting Rows with GREP*

Table 8.5
Utilities that Process Tabular (Row-Column) Data

cut	Deletes columns from a file, producing a new file with shorter lines
paste	Combines the columns of two or more files, producing one file with longer lines that include all the columns in the original files
join	Combines corresponding lines in two files by relating the contents of one or more columns. (This utility implements a relational data base "join" on two tabular files.)

Projecting Columns with *cut*

The **cut** utility deletes columns from a table. For example, suppose a user wanted to project from the **results** file only the columns containing the salesrep, the customer number, and the sale amount. The command

```
$ cut -f1,4,5 results
Jones          Ø221349     6ØØØØ
Jones          Ø213412     57995
Davis          Ø21Ø497      465Ø
Harris         Ø4912Ø7     19425
Harris         Ø421ØØ7     3ØØØØ
Andrews        Ø412Ø95      295Ø
$ ▪
```

will select these columns (identified as the first, fourth, and fifth fields, with the option **-f1,4,5** on the command line). The specified columns are copied to the standard output file. Figure 8.9 illustrates the action of **cut**.

Combining Tables with *paste*

The **paste** utility takes two tables and combines them, side by side, to form a single, wide table as output. The lines of the input files must therefore be in corresponding order before the **paste** utility can be used. This utility is the opposite of **cut**. Figure 8.10 illustrates the action of **paste**.

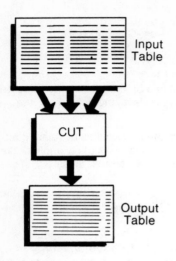

Fig. 8.9. *Projecting Columns with CUT*

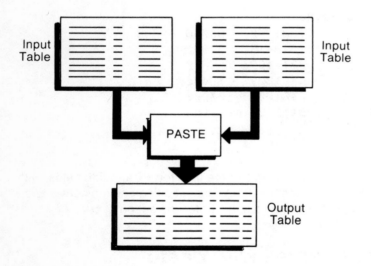

Fig. 8.10. *Combining Tables with PASTE*

Note that the **paste** utility expands a table's width, increasing the number of columns. The **cat** utility, described earlier in this chapter, expands a table's length, increasing the number of rows.

Relating Tables with ***join***

The **join** utility combines data from two tables that contain related information. For example, suppose that the **results** file is to be augmented by adding the name of the appropriate sales office manager to each line of the file. A second file, named **office**, holds a table of sales offices and office managers in two columns:

newyork   **Johnson**
boston   **Anderson**
phila   **Smith**

The **join** utility can be used to create the desired file, matching rows from the two tables, based on the field that is common to both (in this example, the sales office). For each row in the **results** table, the corresponding row in the **office** table (the row with the same sales office) is located. An output row is then created, containing all the columns of the first table and all the columns of the second table. Options to the **join** utility allow the user to choose only certain columns from each table for inclusion in the output table. Figure 8.11 illustrates the action of **join**.

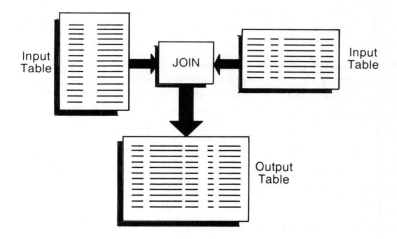

Fig. 8.11. *Relating Tables with JOIN*

The **join** utility is a powerful tool for cross-referencing data from file to file. To process files for reporting, this utility is often used in conjunction with the **cut**, **paste**, **sort**, **split**, and **grep** utilities. These utilities, in fact, implement the features of a relational data base management system for processing tabular files. The relational *selection* operation is implemented by the **grep** utility. The *projection* operation is implemented by the **cut** utility. The relational *join* operation is implemented by the **join** utility. Although the utilities fall short of the sophistication of commercial data base management packages, the utilities offer a convenient relational facility for processing small tables.

Compressing and Encrypting Files

Generally, data files are stored on the UNIX system as plain ASCII text. This storing method simplifies processing since many of the UNIX utilities are most effectively used on text files or on files organized as tables. However, storing files in this manner wastes space. In particular, files will typically contain many sequences of blanks, with each blank character consuming a byte of disk storage. It is not unusual for as much as 30 percent of a file's storage to be consumed in storing these blank characters.

The **pack** utility compacts a file into less disk space by encoding its contents. The details of how files are compressed are not important here, only that a file's storage requirements will usually be reduced significantly by packing. However, once a file has been packed, its contents will be unintelligible to the standard UNIX utilities. A companion utility, **unpack**, returns the file to its original state. Packing is normally used on very large files that are infrequently used since unpacking the files for use can be a time-consuming operation.

If the contents of a file are especially sensitive, an extra measure of security is offered by encrypting the file. The **crypt** utility encodes a file's contents. It uses a user-supplied encryption key to transform the input file, character by character, into the coded output file. To reconstruct the original, uncoded data, the output file is decoded by again using the **crypt** utility.

As with a packed file, the coded file is unintelligible to the standard UNIX utilities. As a result, encoding is usually reserved for files that are used infrequently or for occasions when security is extremely critical, since encoded files must first be decoded for processing.

Table 8.6 describes the data compression and encryption utilities.

Table 8.6
File Compression and Encryption Utilities

crypt	Encodes a file's contents, using a user-supplied encryption key, and decodes encrypted files
makekey	Generates an encryption key for use in programs that must perform encoding/decoding
pack	Generates a "packed" version of a file, which takes less disk space
pcat	Concatenates the contents of several packed files (like the **cat** utility)
unpack	Reconstructs the contents of the original file from a file that has been packed

Text Processing and Office Support

The UNIX system provides a comprehensive set of tools for document preparation and office automation. UNIX text-processing utilities support creation, editing, and formatting of documents. These documents may include text, tabular data, and even mathematical equations. Other utilities support personal office tasks, such as messaging, appointment scheduling, calculation, and graphic data analysis.

The strong UNIX emphasis on text processing is not surprising since one of the earliest applications of UNIX within the Bell System was document preparation. Another major application of UNIX has been software development, which also requires strong text-processing tools. It has been said (only partially in jest) that the UNIX system is really nothing but a very complicated text processor. This chapter describes the UNIX utilities that support text processing and office automation.

Text-Processing and Office Automation Facilities

UNIX supports text processing and office automation through a group of approximately thirty utility programs, which include the following:

- *Text editors.* The standard UNIX system includes both a line editor and a full-screen editor; other editors and word processors have been developed by third parties over the years.

155

- *Text formatters.* These tools transform text prepared with the UNIX text editors into formatted documents, such as letters, manuscripts, and manuals. The text-formatting tools work with a range of printing devices, from draft-quality printers to phototypesetters.

- *Text-processing aids.* UNIX utilities correct spelling errors, aid in hyphenation, produce indexes, and perform other text-processing functions.

- *Calculators.* UNIX utilities simulate calculators with advanced features, such as memory registers, programmability, and programming language constructs.

- *Electronic mail.* An electronic mail facility lets users send messages to other users. Mail can be sent between users on the same system or across the telephone network to users of other systems.

- *Calendar services.* A calendar facility provides appointment tracking and reminder services that adapt to different styles of appointment scheduling.

- *Graphics.* A family of utilities transforms and analyzes data and generates graphics output, such as pie charts, bar charts, scattergrams, and text slides. The utilities support graphics terminals, printers, and plotters.

Text-Processing Tools

The UNIX text-processing tools are a family of utilities that aid in all phases of document preparation. Figure 9.1 shows the phases of the document preparation process.

The UNIX text editors are used to enter the text of a document into the system and store it as a file. The same editors are later used to revise the document, by adding, modifying, and deleting text. The two most popular UNIX editing utilities are **ed**, a line-oriented editor, and **vi**, a screen-oriented editor.

When a document is ready for printing, the UNIX text-formatting utilities control its appearance on the printed page. Formatting commands, included in the text file itself, direct how the unformatted text will be formed into paragraphs, pages, and sections of a document. The **nroff** utility formats text for printing on typewriter-like printing devices, such as draft-quality printers, letter-quality printers, and line printers.

A companion utility, **troff**, formats text for printing on high-resolution printing devices, such as phototypesetters and laser printers. Other utilities handle

Text Entry & Editing

Text Formatting & Printing

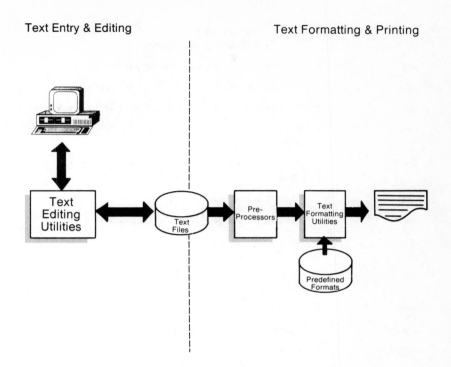

Fig. 9.1. *Text Processing with UNIX*

specialized formatting tasks, such as printing tables and mathematical equations. These latter utilities are used as preprocessors to the main formatting programs.

Many of the file-processing commands described in the previous chapter are useful in combination with the text-editing and text-formatting utilities. The same utilities used to process tables of sales data, for example, can be applied equally well to files containing pages of a technical manual. Table 9.1 lists the most commonly used UNIX text-processing utilities.

The UNIX Line Editor

The **ed** (**ed**itor) utility is the standard UNIX text editor, available on virtually all versions of the UNIX system. This utility is a *command-oriented* editor—it accepts editing commands from the user and performs the requested editing operations on the contents of a text file. The **ed** utility is also *line-oriented*. Its editing commands operate on a single line at a time or on a

Table 9.1
Text-Processing Utilities

ed	Edits a text file, using line-oriented editing
vi	Edits a text file, using screen-oriented editing
pr	Prints a text file with simple headers and page breaks
nroff	Formats text for printing on character-oriented printing devices
troff	Formats text for printing on high-resolution printing devices
tbl	Formats tabular data
eqn	Formats mathematical text and equations
cw	Formats text in a typewriter-style font for printing on high-resolution printing devices
mm	Formats common office documents, such as letters and memoranda
mmt	Formats text for viewgraphs
deroff	Removes formatting commands from a text file
spell	Corrects spelling errors
hyphen	Finds hyphenated words in a text file
diffmk	Compares two versions of a file and produces a version with "change bars"
ptx	Produces a permuted index

range of lines. This text editor is useful for editing documents and other kinds of text stored in UNIX files.

A user's interaction with **ed** takes the form of a dialogue. Like the shell, **ed** prompts the user for a command, accepts it, and carries it out before asking the user for the next command. During an editing session, **ed** stores the text being edited in an *editing buffer* in main memory. If an existing file is to be edited, its contents are first read from the disk into the buffer. When editing is complete, **ed** places the edited text from the buffer back onto the disk.

The editing commands available with **ed** offer a variety of editing functions, such as adding and deleting lines of text, changing text throughout a document, and moving lines of text from one position to another. Editing commands take the form of a single character. For example, the **p** command prints lines of text on the terminal display, and the **m** command moves a group of lines. Table 9.2 lists the most commonly used commands.

Table 9.2
Commonly Used ED Editing Commands

Adding text:

a	Adds new lines
i	Inserts new lines
r	Reads the contents of a file

Modifying text:

d	Deletes lines
c	Replaces (changes) lines
m	Moves lines
t	Copies (duplicates) lines
j	Joins two lines to make one long line
k	Marks a line for later reference
s	Substitutes one piece of text for another

Printing text:

p	Prints lines on the terminal display
ń	Prints lines, along with their line numbers
l	Prints lines, including nonprinting control characters

Miscellaneous:

h	Displays help messages on the terminal display
u	"Undoes" the effects of the last command
!	Executes a shell command from within the editor
w	Writes a copy of the text, including editing changes, into a text file
q	Terminates the editing session

Each editing command operates on a single line or on a range of lines. The user selects the lines to be affected by each command. For example, the user may request that each occurrence of the word "Jim" be changed to "James" in lines 2 through 24 of a document. The user can also use pattern matching and arithmetic to select a range of lines for editing. For instance, a user can instruct **ed** to find the word "contract" in a document and delete the next ten lines, all in a single editing command.

The pattern-matching capabilities available for selecting lines to edit are quite comprehensive. Typical pattern searches may include the following:

- Exact matching of a string of characters

- Wild-card matching of one or more characters

- Matching of text only at the beginning or end of a line

The **ed** utility can be instructed to search either forward or backward through the text to find matching lines. Figure 9.2 illustrates a short editing session.

```
$ ed                                # invoke ed
r results                           # read results into buffer
36Ø                                 # ed indicates file length
4,5p                                # print lines 4 and 5
Harris      newyork    east     Ø491207   19425
Harris      newyork    east     Ø421007   3ØØØØ
4,5s/Harris/Greene/                 # substitute text
4,5p                                # print lines 4 and 5 again
Greene      newyork    east     Ø491207   19425
Greene      newyork    east     Ø421007   3ØØØØ
w                                   # write the modified text to disk
36Ø                                 # file length hasn't changed
q                                   # exit the editing session
$ ■
```

Fig. 9.2. *A Sample ED Editing Session*

This utility is limited to editing text files that fit in their entirety into the main memory editing buffer. Longer documents may be broken into sections or chapters for editing, with each section stored in its own text file. File-processing utilities can be used to split apart a large file for editing and then reassemble it for printing. If a very large file must be edited directly, the UNIX stream editor, **sed**, may be used. This utility is described in Chapter 8.

Screen-Oriented Editing with **vi**

The **vi** (visual editor) utility is an interactive, screen-oriented editor that has become very popular among UNIX users. Like the **ed** editor, **vi** copies the contents of a text file into a buffer in main memory for editing. However, **vi** uses the terminal display as a "window" into the buffer, showing approximately twenty lines of text on the display at all times. On command, the window can be moved up and down through the buffer so that the user can examine the entire contents of the buffer. Figure 9.3 shows how the terminal display and editing buffer interact when **vi** is used.

To edit text, the user simply moves the cursor about the display, using the single-character commands. These commands also move the cursor forward and backward through the text—a character, a word, a sentence, or a line at a time. Other editing commands are used to insert, modify, and delete

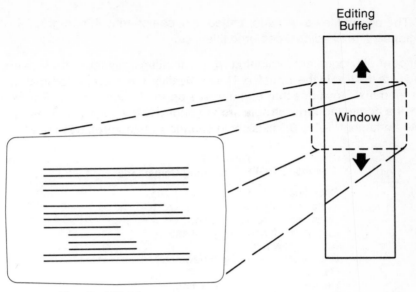

Fig. 9.3. *Editing with VI*

text. The command specifies whether editing is to be performed on a character, a word, or a line. The results of each editing command are immediately reflected on the terminal display.

In addition to editing text directly on the terminal display, **vi** includes a set of editing commands similar to those available with the **ed** utility. These **vi** commands make mass changes to an entire document or to ranges of lines within the document. Again, **vi** immediately updates the displayed text to reflect each editing command.

Developed at Berkeley, the **vi** editor has become a popular addition to the various versions of UNIX. The utility is now included as a standard part of the UNIX System V. The **vi** editor has been integrated with the **terminfo** facility so that the user can take advantage of special terminal features, such as cursor control and function keys.

Text Formatting with *nroff*

The **nroff** (**new run**off) utility formats the contents of a text file for printing. The utility accepts a text file as input and produces a formatted document, ready for printing, as its output file. The input file contains text in free format, which can be edited by a user without regard to its final appearance on the printed page. The output file contains formatted text, complete with paragraph indentations, page headings, centered titles, etc.

A user controls document formatting with formatting commands that are included with the text in the input file. The **nroff** utility interprets as commands, rather than text, any lines that begin with a period in column one. For example, the command **.bp** instructs **nroff** to begin a new page when formatting the document. Table 9.3 lists some commonly used **nroff** commands.

Table 9.3
Common NROFF Formatting Commands

.ad l	Specifies left justification
.ad r	Specifies right justification
.ad c	Specifies center justification
.ad b	Specifies left and right justification
.bp	Starts a new page
.br	Breaks text, beginning a new line
.ce	Centers text
.de	Defines a text-processing macro
.fi	Turns on text filling
.hw	Specifies word hyphenation
.hy	Turns on hyphenation
.in	Indents a paragraph
.ll	Sets line length
.ls	Sets line spacing
.na	Turns off text adjusting (justification)
.ne	Keeps text together on a single page
.nf	Turns off text filling
.nh	Turns off hyphenation
.pl	Sets page length
.po	Sets page offset
.pn	Sets page number
.sp	Produces blank lines
.ti	Indents a single line
.tl	Specifies a three-part title
.ul	Underlines text
.wh	Sets traps for macro processing

One of the most often used **nroff** functions is text justification. The **nroff** utility arranges text within user-specified margins on the page. At the user's option, **nroff** can left-justify or right-justify text, or both. Other capabilities of **nroff** include the following:

- Automatic page header/footer printing
- Automatic footnoting
- Automatic section numbering
- Multicolumn printing

- Line spacing and line length control

- Line indentation

Figure 9.4 shows a simple text file with embedded formatting commands and the resulting output when the file is processed by **nroff**.

Input text file:

```
.ll 50                          # set line length of 50
.ce 2                           # center next 2 lines
.cu 2                           # underline next 2 lines
Sales Analysis by Region
November, 1983
.sp 2                           # skip 2 lines
.ti 5                           # indent next line 5 spaces
November proved to be an excellent month,
with all regions once again turning in good
sales performances.
Special recognition is due to
John Davis
in the
Boston
office, who led the sales force in orders.
```

Formatted output file:

```
              Sales Analysis by Region
                 November, 1983


     November proved to be an excellent month,
with all regions once again turning in good sales
performances. Special recognition is due to John
Davis in the Boston office, who led the sales force
in orders.
```

Fig. 9.4. *An NROFF Formatting Example*

Phototypesetting with troff

Troff (typesetter **runoff**) offers the same basic set of formatting functions as **nroff**, but with expanded capabilities to support high-resolution printing devices. These devices can print text in different fonts, including roman, italic, and bold characters; and greek and special math characters. The **troff** utility also gives the user control over type size and supports proportional spaced printing.

Text-Formatting Macros

The **nroff** and **troff** utilities provide very precise control over the appearance of printed output. However, using these utilities directly is a tedious operation, since several commands are required to specify simple functions that are used again and again, such as "start a new paragraph by skipping a line and indenting 5 spaces."

To provide a higher level of support for common document processing, several macro packages have been developed. These packages offer predefined formatting commands. In place of several **nroff** commands, the macro packages provide single commands for functions like page numbering, setting up a table of contents, formatting a memory, forming the salutation, and closing a business letter, etc. Most users use **nroff** and **troff** through these macro packages, instead of using the utilities directly.

Specialized Text Formatting

Documents produced with the text-processing utilities will often include tabular data. The **tbl** (**table** formatter) utility formats tabular data of up to 35 columns for printing by the **nroff** or **troff** formatters. **Tbl** is a filter, used as a preprocessor for these utilities. As with **nroff** and **troff**, the user controls the **tbl** utility through formatting commands embedded in the text file.

The printed appearance of a table within a document can be controlled through **tbl** commands that perform the following tasks:

- Left- or center-justify the table in the document
- Enclose the table in a box or double box
- Expand the table to fill the width of a text line
- Enclose each item of the table in a box

Detailed control over the format of each column in the table is also available through formatting commands that specify the following:

- Type font
- Type size
- Column width

- Left/right/center/numeric justification
- Text spanning across several columns

Figure 9.5 shows a file with **tbl** commands, along with the resulting output.

Input text file:

```
.TS                     # start table
allbox;                 # enclose each table element in a box
c s s s s               # center first line and span all columns
c c c c c               # center each column in second line
l l l l n               # left and numeric justifications
Sales Results
Salesman  Office    Region    Customer    Amount
Jones     boston    east      0221349     60000
Jones     boston    east      0213412     57995
Davis     boston    east      0210497     4650
Harris    newyork   east      0491207     19425
Harris    newyork   east      0421007     30000
Andrews   phila     east      0412095     2950
.TE                     # end of table
```

Formatted output file:

Sales Results				
Salesman	Office	Region	Customer	Amount
Jones	boston	east	0221349	60000
Jones	boston	east	0213412	57995
Davis	boston	east	0210497	4650
Harris	newyork	east	0491207	19425
Harris	newyork	east	0421007	30000
Andrews	phila	east	0412095	2950

Fig. 9.5. *A TBL Formatting Example*

Another utility, **eqn** (**eq**uation formatter) is used to format mathematical equations that include special symbols.

Calculation Tools

The **dc** (**d**esktop **c**alculator) utility is a general-purpose calculating tool. The utility simulates a handheld calculator that uses *reverse polish* notation, as in those marketed by Hewlett-Packard. This kind of calculator stores calculation results on a "push-down stack," which is particularly useful for chain calculations in which the result of one calculation step is used in subsequent steps. The **dc** calculator offers over a hundred memory registers to store intermediate calculation results for later use. Table 9.4 lists the operations available with **dc**.

Table 9.4
Desktop Calculator Features

Arithmetic operations:

+	Addition
−	Subtraction
*	Multiplication
/	Division
%	Remainder (after division)
^	Exponentiation (x to the power y)
v	Square root

Commands:

p	Prints the top of stack
s	Stores the top of stack in a memory register
l	Recalls a memory register onto the top of stack
f	Prints the contents of the stack and registers
d	Duplicates the value on the top of stack
c	Clears the stack

The **dc** utility automatically handles arbitrarily large or small numbers in its calculations, with no loss of accuracy. Unlike typical desktop calculators, which store numbers internally to an accuracy of 8 or 14 digits, **dc** automatically adjusts its internal storage methods to store each number as precisely as possible. This feature can be very important when calculating, for example, with interest rates computed to thousandths of a percent in combination with account balances of millions of dollars. Normally, **dc** accepts input and displays its results in decimal (base 10) notation. For convenience to programmers, however, **dc** can also work in octal (base 8) and hexadecimal (base 16) notation. Figure 9.6 shows a short **dc** calculation to compute the circumference and area of a circle.

Given a circle, what is its circumference and area?

$ **dc**	# shell command invokes the desk calculator
3.1416	# enter the value of "pi"
sA	# store it in register "A" for later recall
7.5	# enter the radius
sB	# store it in register "B" for later recall
lB	# recall radius from register "B"
2	# enter the number 2
*	# multiply 2 x radius to get diameter
lA	# recall "pi"
*	# multiply "pi" x diameter to get circumference
p	# print result
47.191	
lB	# recall radius from register "B"
d	# duplicate top of stack
*	# multiply to get radius squared
lA	# recall "pi"
*	# multiply to get area
p	# print the result
176.715	

Fig. 9.6. *Sample DC Calculation*

The **dc** calculator is also programmable. A sequence of keystrokes (single-character commands, entered numbers, etc.) can be stored in one of the calculator's memory registers and later executed automatically with a single command. Results of calculations can also be tested within a program, to execute different instructions based on these results. This feature is especially useful when the same calculation must be repeated over and over again on different data.

A companion utility, **bc**, offers even more programmability. This utility adds programming language constructs to the basic calculation features of **dc**. The **bc** utility is comparable in programming power to the simpler versions of the BASIC language. The utility's programming language constructs include the following:

- Variables with single-character names

- Begin/end blocks

- Conditional testing (**if ... then**)

- Looping (**while ...**)

- Iteration (**for ...**)
- Multiline functions

Two other UNIX utilities offer specialized calculation support. The **units** utility performs conversion for scientific and engineering calculations, such as centimeters-to-inches and pounds-to-kilograms calculations. The **factor** utility factors a number into its prime number factors.

The Mail Facility

The **mail** utility provides the ability to send and receive electronic mail among users of a UNIX system. This facility lacks the sophistication of a formal electronic mail software package, but **mail** does offer a simple, effective, and often used communication tool. Using the UNIX communications facilities, the mail facility can send mail to users of other UNIX systems over the public telephone network.

Users send mail to other users on the same UNIX system by user name. Mail can also be sent to users on other UNIX systems by giving both the name of the system and the user's name on that system. A configuration file maintained by the system administrator is used to locate the remote system. An exclamation point is used to indicate a remote system name. The name

  boston!joe

refers to the user named **joe** on the **boston** system.

The mail facility can even route mail through one or more intermediate systems to its final destination. The name

  boston!newyork!henry

refers to the user **henry** on the **newyork** system, which is reached by sending mail through the **boston** system.

For short messages the **mail** utility can be used to enter interactively the text of the message. Input text is taken from the terminal, as in the following example:

```
$ mail joe sam
Did you receive the report from accounting last week? Our depart-
ments were 10% over budget, and we need to discuss the situation.
Please call me today.--George

$ ▪
```

Longer messages can be prepared with one of the UNIX text editors and stored in a text file. Redirecting the mail command's standard input to this file will transmit the message. For example, the command

```
$  mail joe sam <memo
$  ■
```

will send as mail the text file **memo** to users **joe** and **sam**.

Each user of the system has a separate *mailbox* to receive incoming mail. The **mail** utility is also used to examine the mailbox and dispose of incoming mail. Each message in the mailbox is presented on the screen, with the most recently received message being displayed first. The **mail** utility pauses after displaying each message, offering several options for disposing of it. The user may do one of the following:

- Go on to the next message
- Go back to the previous message
- Delete the message
- Display the message again
- Save the message in a file for further processing
- Forward the message to one or more users

As with many UNIX utilities, the user may also execute a shell command from within the **mail** facility. This ability allows the user to take immediate action on incoming mail, for example, by printing a report or starting a program.

A newer version of the **mail** utility, called **mailx**, offers several important extensions of the UNIX mail facility. The **mailx** utility accepts more than fifty commands that control editing, sending, receiving, and processing of mail. Using these commands, the user can

- Establish for a group of users an *alias*, which can be used like a distribution list
- Invoke an editor from within the mail facility in order to edit messages
- Use a single command to operate on groups of messages, identified by message number, author, subject matter, and so on
- Pipe mail messages to a shell command for processing and incorporate command output or other files into a mail message

- Respond to incoming mail messages, with the mail facility automatically handling distribution of the reply message, electronic carbon copies, and so on

The **mailx** facility also gives the user considerable flexibility in tailoring a personal electronic mail environment. More than forty different environment variables can be set to customize the operation of **mailx**. In addition, system-wide and personal start-up files (named **.mailrc**) are executed automatically when **mailx** begins operation, providing further opportunity for automatic or custom processing.

Calendar and Reminder Services

A pair of UNIX utilities provides an on-line calendar and a reminder service for office support. The **cal** utility prints a calendar for any month or year requested by the user, offering a convenient way to look up future and past dates without leaving the terminal. The **cal** operation is very straightforward, as illustrated here:

```
$ cal 11 1983
      November 1983
 S   M  Tu  W  Th   F   S
         1   2   3   4   5
 6   7   8   9  1Ø  11  12
13  14  15  16  17  18  19
2Ø  21  22  23  24  25  26
27  28  29  3Ø

$ ■
```

The **calendar** utility implements a simple reminder service for UNIX users. It scans a *calendar file* and displays lines that contain either today's date or tomorrow's date. The utility recognizes common methods of representing dates (for example, it finds 10/14, Oct. 14, and October 14).

In typical UNIX style, the **calendar** utility offers users flexibility in formatting their reminder messages. Appointments are stored in free form in the calendar file, with one appointment per line. As long as the appointment date appears somewhere in the line, the **calendar** utility will locate it successfully. All other details (such as information stored about each appointment, order of fields on the line, and length of the line) are left to the user's discretion.

Thus, each user on the system can have his own personal method for organizing a calendar and still use one common utility program to receive reminders.

The Message Facility

In usual daily operation, a UNIX system will have many users at terminals located throughout an organization. Some users may even use the system remotely over telephone lines. The message facility offers a quick and easy service for sending short messages between users who are logged in.

The **write** utility sends a message to another user. After giving the name of the user for whom the message is destined, the utility accepts input from the sender, line by line. To send a short message to user **george**, the user named **sam** types the following:

```
$ write george
I need to see you before lunch today to discuss the McPherson
deal. How about 11:30?--sam
$ ▪
```

The message is terminated by typing the *end-of-file* character (**Control-D**) and is displayed by the **write** utility on the receiving user's terminal, line by line, as the sender types the message. An introductory line identifies the source of the message.

```
Message from sam tty 1Ø...
I need to see you before lunch today to discuss the
McPherson deal. How about 11:3Ø?--sam
EOF
```

At times, receiving unsolicited messages from another user can be a great inconvenience. For example, if a user is in the middle of editing a carefully formatted text document when a message arrives, the message will appear on the screen in the midst of the document text, disturbing its appearance. The UNIX system allows a user to control receipt of messages from other users with the **mesg** utility. The command

```
$ mesg n
$ ■
```

prevents further receipt of messages until the user decides to accept them once again, with the following command:

```
$ mesg y
$ ■
```

The On-line Newsletter

The UNIX utility **news** implements an on-line newsletter for users of the system. News files are prepared by using the standard text-editing tools and are placed in a special directory named **/usr/news**. To see current news items, the user runs the **news** utility. Items are displayed for review, with the most recent item displayed first. This utility is a simple, but effective, way of improving office communications.

Options to the **news** utility permit quick perusal of news items. The user can request only a count of the number of news items or ask for a listing of only the titles of the news items. Particular news items of interest can also be selected individually. In systems where **news** is extensively used to keep users up-to-date on current information, the **news** command is often included in the **/etc/profile** file, causing it to be automatically executed whenever a user first logs into the system.

The Graphics Facility

UNIX includes a graphics subsystem that assists with analysis and presentation of numerical information. A family of specialized utilities provides the graphics functions. Typically, several utilities are joined with UNIX pipes to accomplish a complete graphics task. Figure 9.7 shows a typical example, in which a file containing laboratory test results is transformed into a histogram, graphically showing their distribution.

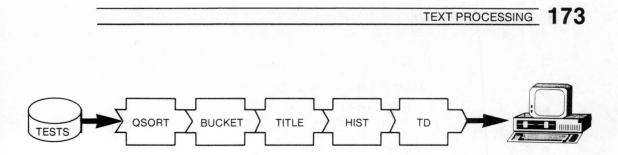

Fig. 9.7. *Using the Graphics Utilities*

In the figure, the file **tests** contains the test results, stored as a sequence of numbers. The data is sorted into sequence, using the **qsort** graphics utility. The sorted results are piped to the **bucket** utility, which classifies the results into ranges and then counts the results. The **title** utility adds a title to the data, and the **hist** utility produces a histogram. Finally, the **td** utility plots the histogram on a graphics display terminal. The sequence of five filter programs transforms the raw test results into a graphic presentation that aids analysis of the data.

A collection of statistical utilities, known as the *statistical network*, supports numeric computation on data to be graphed. The utilities are used to generate number sequences, perform arithmetic calculations on them, calculate statistics, and transform sequences into graphical representations. Table 9.5 lists the graphics and statistical utilities available.

Table 9.5
Graphics Utilities

Generating number sequences:

gas	Generates arithmetic sequences
prime	Generates prime number sequences
rand	Generates random number sequences

Sequence transformation:

abs	Absolute value
mod	Modulo (remainder)
round	Round
ceil	Round up
floor	Round down
exp, log, gamma	Exponentials and logarithms
power, root	Powers and roots
af	Arbitrary arithmetic formulas
cusum	Cumulative sum
siline	Line fitting
spline	Curve fitting

Table 9.5 *(continued)*

sin	Trig functions
subset	Subset selection
qsort, rank	Sorting and ordering
prod	Internal products

Statistics:

mean	Average (arithmetic mean)
total	Total
hilo	Minimum and maximum
bucket	Classification into ranges
cor	Correlation coefficient
lreg	Linear regression
var	Variance

Graphics:

bar	Bar charts
pie	Pie charts
plot	X/Y line charts and scattergrams
hist	Histograms
title	Chart titles
label	Chart axis labels

Users may also use the **ged** (**g**raphics **ed**itor) utility to manipulate graphics elements (such as text, lines, and circles) on a graphics display. With **ged**, users can construct drawings and modify them until they have the desired appearance. Commands are available to perform the following tasks:

- Position graphics text on the screen

- Draw straight lines

- Draw arcs, boxes, and circles

- Move objects about the screen

- Change the shape and size of an object

- Rotate an object

The graphics editor, in combination with the statistical network utilities, gives the user nearly total control over formatting of graphics output produced by UNIX. Additional utilities plot this output on popular graphics output devices, such as graphics terminals, dot-matrix printers, and plotters.

10

Software Development

T he UNIX system has always enjoyed an excellent reputation as a software development tool. In fact, many computer science experts claim that UNIX, along with the C programming language, is the best environment available for developing complex systems and applications software products. Most of the leading suppliers of microcomputer software—including Microsoft, Digital Research, VisiCorp®, MicroPro®, and others—develop software in C under UNIX. The UNIX/C combination is even popular for developing software that will run on mainframe systems and on microcomputers that do not themselves run UNIX. In this "cross development" environment, programmers use UNIX to develop software for applications as diverse as computer games, robotics, and electronic test equipment.

Providing an excellent environment for serious software development was one of the goals of the UNIX system from the very beginning. Software development was the major UNIX application within Bell Labs, where UNIX was created. UNIX also plays a major role in computer science education in colleges and universities, where UNIX's popularity grew in the 1970s. Over 80 percent of the colleges that award computer science degrees are AT&T licensees for the UNIX system. It is difficult for a student to earn a degree in computer science today without substantial exposure to UNIX and its concepts. In fact, the universities have been turning out a steady stream of UNIX enthusiasts, who have formed the core of the UNIX popularity boom of the last few years.

This chapter describes the UNIX system's programming tools and how they work together to make UNIX a superior environment for serious software development.

The UNIX Software Development Environment

The UNIX features that support software development include most of the capabilities described previously in this book. The hierarchical UNIX file system, for example, offers a natural way to organize the thousands of individual files required to support a programming team. Program source code, test files, development tools, and object programs can all be organized to support effective individual work by each programmer, yet they offer sharing of common modules and tools. Similarly, programmers use the UNIX file-processing and text-processing utilities extensively to create, edit, and test programs, and to connect them together into complete applications systems.

The following features of the UNIX system are specifically targeted to support effective software development by a team of programmers:

- *The C programming language.* UNIX and C are intimately connected, with many UNIX facilities particularly well suited to C programming. C offers an excellent compromise between demands for a high-level language that makes a programmer efficient and a low-level language that gives the programmer direct access to hardware features.

- *The software tools approach.* The structure of UNIX encourages programmers to develop tools that assist in the development process. Spending the time to develop a specialized software tool that speeds subsequent development is a time-honored practice in UNIX software development. The UNIX pipe structure also allows programmers to create these new tools by connecting existing tools in new ways.

- *The Source Code Control System (SCCS).* SCCS helps to manage and coordinate software development by a team of programmers working on interrelated projects. With SCCS, changes to a large pool of software source code can be carefully managed and tracked, keeping team software development coordinated and under control.

- *Libraries.* UNIX maintains system-defined and user-defined libraries of software routines that perform commonly needed application functions. By including these routines into new programs, programmers can cut development time and ensure consistency across a wide body of software.

- *Communications tools.* UNIX systems are often used as development tools for software that will execute on other, non-UNIX systems. UNIX communications utilities, described in Chapter 11, allow software developed on a UNIX system to be effectively downloaded to other systems for testing and execution.

The C Programming Language

The histories of the UNIX system and the C programming language are closely linked, and there is a special relationship between the operating system and the programming language. UNIX itself is almost exclusively written in C. Thus, UNIX exists only on systems that have C compilers. Several general-purpose UNIX utilities, such as **awk** and **bc**, accept commands that are modeled on C programming language features. Other utilities, such as **lint**, are specifically targeted to support software development in C.

The primary reason for the popularity of the C programming language is its excellent compromise between two opposite, but important, demands commonly placed on programming languages. *Efficiency for programmers* is needed to maximize programmer effectiveness when developing new software. *Efficiency for computers* is needed in the resulting software so that it performs well when it is executed.

Many studies have shown that a programmer tends to produce the same number of lines of debugged program text, regardless of the programming language being used. Higher-level programming languages are, therefore, preferred for software development. Since each line in a higher-level programming language can express a more complex operation than a line in a lower-level language, applications programs written in higher-level languages are shorter and take less time to develop. These programs are also easier to understand and debug.

But higher-level languages can be wasteful and produce inefficient programs. Because the programmer is far removed from the details of the computer's hardware features, the programs produced by a higher-level language cannot make maximum use of these features in the computer instructions that they produce. It is not unusual for a higher-level language to produce a program that is three or even five times as large as a program that is custom-written in a low-level, assembly language by an expert programmer. The performance of the resulting programs can also differ by as much as five to one.

The C language offers programmers an ideal blend of high-level features and low-level efficiency for many programming tasks:

- C is a block-structured programming language that encourages conceptual, top-down programming techniques. Programs are built from functions, which themselves rest on lower-level functions. Altogether, they yield a clear, modular structure.

- C gives programmers low-level control over machine features for developing system software or for performance tuning an application. For example, a programmer can designate variables to be kept in high-performance registers and manipulate directly bit-level data without resorting to assembly language.

- C is flexible, with a variety of data types, a rich set of operators, and a small, but capable, set of programming commands.

- C is a very compact core language, with an extensive library of routines supporting common functions. Users can effectively extend the language by creating their own libraries of user-defined functions.

One of the most important features of C is its portability. Though C offers programmers the power of bit-level data manipulation, the language itself is independent of the arrangement of stacks, registers, and other features of a particular processor. C compilers are available for many systems, from 8-bit microprocessors to mainframes and supercomputers.

The portability of C has been further enhanced by its emerging status as a language standardized by the American National Standards Institute (ANSI). ANSI standards for other languages, such as COBOL and FORTRAN, have made them widely available and compatible across a broad range of computer systems. The ANSI committee responsible for the C standard, X3J11, published a draft standard in August, 1985. This standard has been widely reviewed and, at this writing, the draft seems assured of acceptance as an ANSI standard. Parallel work in the International Standards Organization (ISO) should produce an identical international standard for C at about the same time that the ANSI standard becomes final.

C programs are structured as a collection of functions. Each function is a self-contained module with its own arguments, a return value, and local storage and processing operations. Functions call on other, lower-level functions to perform their work. This structure encourages modular, top-down programming and lends itself naturally to software development by a team of programmers working independently.

Data Types

C supports a variety of data types, for representing naturally different types of data. In addition to the integer, character, and floating-point data types that are typical of all languages, C offers compound data types as well. *Arrays* of data provide an effective way to organize tables and lists. *Structures* are used to group together related data items into a single entity. For example, the individual pieces of data available for a customer—name, address, account balance, etc.—can be combined into a structure and manipulated individually or as a unit in C. *Pointers* are used to identify the location of stored data and to form relationships among data elements. Using these data types, programmers can organize data in the way that is most natural for the application, instead of programming the application to fit a data organization dictated by the language.

Storage Classes

C offers the following types of data storage for data that is used in separate modules of a program:

- *Automatic* variables store data that is used only within a function. These variables are initialized each time the function is called and usually take up main memory space only when the function itself is executing.

- *Static* variables also contain private data that is used only within a function. But unlike automatic variables, static variables retain their previous values each time a function is called. A static variable is used, for example, to hold a count of how many times a function has been called.

- *External* variables contain data that is defined outside a function, but which may be accessed and modified from within the function.

- *Register* variables give programmers a tool for performance tuning their programs. They are identified to the C compiler as variables that are frequently used and, therefore, good candidates for storing in a computer's high-speed register hardware.

Because C is a portable language, there is no guarantee that register variables will, in fact, be stored in high-performance memory locations. However, the register storage class provides a hardware-independent method for identifying this kind of data in the language.

Operators

The C language includes a rich assortment of operators to compute, manipulate, and compare data. The normal arithmetic operations are augmented with bit-level operators that perform logical operations and bit-level tests, and shift data. Auto-incrementing and auto-decrementing operations are also supported, offering programmers a natural way to process lists, arrays, and counts. Assignment operations are very flexible, with assignment operators combining arithmetic, logical, and auto-incrementing operations and value assignment in a single operation. The largest assortment of operators available makes C programs more difficult to read for the novice, but provides the experienced programmer with a compact, efficient way to express required computations.

Table 10.1 summarizes the main structures of the C programming language.

Table 10.1
C Programming Language Features

Data Types:

- Character
- Integer (long and short)
- Floating point (long and short)
- Array
- Pointer
- Structure (composite data type)
- Enumeration (set of values)

Storage Classes:

- Automatic
- Static
- External
- Register

Unary Operations:

- Negation
- Complement
- Logical negation
- Indirection
- Pointer
- Pre- and post-increment
- Pre- and post-decrement

Table 10.1 *(continued)*

Binary operations:

- Addition
- Subtraction
- Multiplication
- Division
- Remainder
- Bit-shifting (right/left)
- Bit-by-bit AND, OR, Exclusive OR

Relational tests:

- Equal
- Not equal
- Greater than
- Greater than or equal
- Less than
- Less than or equal

Functions:

- Return a single, typed value
- Call-by-value arguments (except for arrays)

Statement types:

- Simple statement
- Block ({ ... })
- Conditional (**if ..., if ..., else ...**)
- Looping (**while ..., do ... while ...**)
- Iteration (**for ...**)
- Selection (**switch ...**)
- Branching (**goto ...**)

Compiler directives:

- Symbolic constant definition
- Inclusion of source text from a library
- Conditional compilation

Libraries

Libraries extend the power of the UNIX programming languages. A *library* is a collection of preprogrammed functions that perform specific, commonly needed tasks. These functions may be referenced in a program, and they are automatically linked into the program when it is prepared for execution. With these functions, programmers can tap the wealth of software already developed for the UNIX system and avoid duplication of effort. Functions in the library are called within a program just as if they had been written by the programmer.

The UNIX system has three standard libraries. To support other functions, users can expand these libraries or add their own libraries. For example, most data base management software packages include a library of functions for data base access from C programs. When this library is installed on the system, the functions are called by programs that access the data base.

The *C library*, supplied with the C language, is a collection of functions that extend C's capabilities. Over one hundred functions in this library give programmers convenient routines to perform the following:

- File input/output and status checking
- String manipulation, such as comparison and searching
- Character processing and testing for digits, upper- and lower-case, etc.
- Date and time operations
- Numerical conversion from integers to floating point, etc.
- Encryption
- Access to the system's group and password files
- Processing of command options and shell variables
- Tables searching for hash tables, binary trees, and lists
- Memory allocation and de-allocation
- Random number generation

The *object file library* is a collection of functions for manipulating compiled (object) programs. This library is rarely used by applications programmers. Finally, the *mathematical library* is a collection of functions for engineering and scientific calculations within a program, which includes the following:

- Trigonometric functions
- Bessel functions
- Hyperbolic trigonometric functions
- Rounding, absolute value, logarithm, and power functions

Checking C Program Portability

The **lint** utility checks the syntax of C language programs. **Lint** helps programmers ensure that their C programs are transportable to other computer systems. The C programming language, because of its low-level operations, can be used to create programs that are hardware dependent. For example, a programmer may make assumptions about the internal format of a certain data type. These assumptions may be valid on one system, but not on others. The **lint** utility checks a C program using stricter rules than the C compiler and reports on program statements that may cause portability problems. The utility also performs other consistency checks on programs, such as verifying that variables are initialized before they are used, and locating statements that cannot be reached during program execution.

The Symbolic Debugger

The **sdb** utility is a symbolic debugger for programs written in C. Using **sdb**, a programmer can interactively debug a program at the source language level, which is an advantage for quickly locating and correcting programming errors. This utility allows a programmer to examine program behavior step by step. The following features are included in the **sdb** utility:

- *Breakpoints.* Execution is automatically halted when a program reaches a predefined point, for examining the values of the variables, the logical flow of the program, etc.

- *Single step.* Execution takes place one step at a time, for detailed observation of program behavior.

- *Variable examination.* Variable values can be examined during execution while a program is temporarily halted.

- *Source code viewing.* Program source code can be viewed for reference while examining variables, tracing execution, etc.

- *Function call trace.* The sequence of function calls that led a program to a particular instruction can be traced.

- *Function execution.* Functions within the program can be executed individually, to test their proper operation.

Other Program Development Tools

The UNIX system includes a number of other utilities that aid in the program development process. Table 10.2 lists a few of these utilities. Two of the most complex utilities in the UNIX system, **yacc** and **lex**, fall into this category. Both are tools originally designed to help programmers develop systems-level software, but they may also be used in the development of command-oriented applications programs.

Table 10.2
Program Development Utilities

lint	Checks the syntax of C programs
cb	Formats a C program with indentation and spacing
cxref	Generates a C program cross-reference listing
cflow	Produces flow graphs of C, yacc, lex, and asm
sdb	Aids in source code debugging
ld	Links program modules into an object file
od	Generates an octal dump
nm	Prints the symbol table from an object program file
size	Displays the size of object program files
lex	Generates programs to perform lexical analysis
yacc	Aids in development of compilers, interpreters, and complex command-driven programs
lorder	Lists the external identifiers in each object file in a library or archive
strip	Strips symbol table information from an object file
ar	Maintains archives and libraries
m4	Performs macro preprocessing
make	Determines the sequence of steps required to recompile a complex program comprised of many different modules, some of which have been updated

The **lex** (**lex**ical analyzer) utility is used for command language processing. Many useful programs are command driven, requiring that programmers develop software routines to accept a line of text from the user and interpret it as a command with options and arguments. The **lex** utility builds this software automatically. The programmer gives **lex** a set of rules describing the acceptable commands, and **lex** produces routines that perform the lexical analysis of command lines, breaking them into their component pieces.

A companion utility, **yacc** (**y**et **a**nother **c**ompiler **c**ompiler), picks up where **lex** leaves off. Like **lex**, **yacc** produces a set of software routines as its output. The programmer gives **yacc** a set of rules describing the command language and the actions to take when each command or command option is recognized. Then **yacc** translates these specifications into software routines that implement the command language described by the user. The **yacc** and **lex** utilities can be used together to reduce greatly the development time for producing command-driven software products, such as compilers and editors.

Other Language Processors

The standard UNIX system from AT&T includes a C compiler, a version of which is usually supplied by computer manufacturers as a standard part of their system software. Most of these compilers are derived from the same *portable C compiler*, or **pcc**, with modifications to support the particular computer system on which the compilers are being used. The various versions of the UNIX system include several other languages as well, which are listed in Table 10.3. Not all the languages are provided in UNIX versions from minicomputer and microcomputer manufacturers; the individual specifications of each system must be checked to determine whether or not a particular compiler is provided. Independent software suppliers offer additional compilers for COBOL, Pascal, Fortran, PL/I, APL, Ada, BASIC, and many other languages.

Table 10.3
Other Language Processors

as	An assembler for the PDP-11 or VAX-11 processor family
f77	A FORTRAN-77 compiler
ratfor	A compiler for a dialect of FORTRAN
efl	A compiler for an extended FORTRAN language
sno	A SNOBOL interpreter
bs	A compiler for a language that combines features of BASIC, SNOBOL, and C, designed for rapid development
regcmp	A compiler for regular expressions, such as those used in the **ed** and **grep** utilities

The Source Code Control System

The UNIX *Source Code Control System* (SCCS) is a collection of utilities designed to assist the management of large-scale software development projects. Although originally developed to manage files containing program source code, SCCS can be applied equally as well to managing almost any collection of text files. SCCS organizes changes to the files into a series of versions and revisions of the text, allowing users to access the precise version that they need.

SCCS can also restrict changes to the files it manages, permitting only a specific list of users to modify each file. These utilities track each change to a file, recording its purpose, the name of the user who made the change, and the time of the modification. SCCS stores and retrieves different versions of each file, allowing recovery from errors and "roll back" to earlier versions. Most importantly, SCCS prevents several users from trying to change the same version of a file at once.

It is easy to understand SCCS operation by comparing it to a public library. The individual files under SCCS control correspond to the books in the library, with SCCS in the librarian's role. To work any of the files, a user "checks out" the file, and SCCS notes which file was withdrawn, when, and by whom. A file can be withdrawn for examination only, or it can be withdrawn with the intention to revise it. Once withdrawn, a file can be edited and processed, using the normal UNIX text-processing tools. If the file contains program source code, it will likely be compiled, tested, and perhaps recompiled many times over, with intermediate editing sessions.

Normally, SCCS will only allow one user at a time to withdraw any given version of an SCCS file for modification. This limitation prevents multiple users from making conflicting changes to the file. When the user is satisfied with the changes made, the file is returned. SCCS stores the revisions as a new version of the file, along with a user-supplied comment as to why the revisions were made. Changes can be made only to files that were withdrawn for modification.

Figure 10.1 illustrates the role of SCCS in text management. The **get** and **delta** utilities withdraw files from the SCCS pool and introduce altered files back into the pool, respectively.

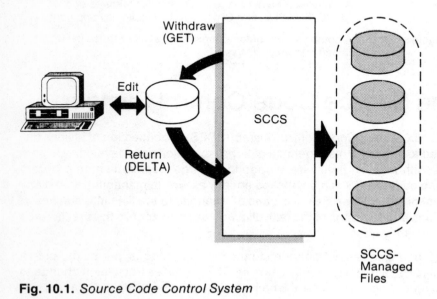

Fig. 10.1. *Source Code Control System*

SCCS Version Control

SCCS stores each file under its control as an "original" file, plus a sequence of updates to the file, called *deltas*, which contain only the modifications made to the file. By organizing its files in this way, SCCS maintains many different versions of each file, using much less disk space than would be required to store each version in its entirety. SCCS numbers the various versions of a file, using a four-level numbering scheme, shown in Figure 10.2. By convention, the *release number* is used to identify major new versions of a text file. Normally, changes are identified by incrementing the *level number*, indicating a new revision within the same release. The original version of each SCCS text file is identified as version 1.1, the next version is version 1.2, and so on.

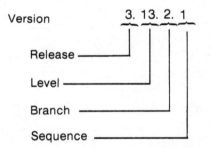

Fig. 10.2. *SCCS Version Numbering*

At times, several different authors will make different modifications to the same version of a text file. SCCS accommodates this by creating a *branch* version of the text, using the remaining two levels of its four-level numbering scheme. Branching can occur over and over again, as shown in Figure 10.3. Note that three different current versions of the text have been developed from a common original text, through different sets of modifications.

SCCS Security

SCCS implements additional security features, beyond those of the UNIX file systems, for tight control over file modification. For each file managed by SCCS, the owner may specify a list of users and/or user groups who are allowed to create new versions of the file. The owner can also lock specific versions of an SCCS file against further modification. These versions can be withdrawn from SCCS for inspection, but cannot be modified. A specific range of versions can also be specified as the only versions of a file that are available for updating.

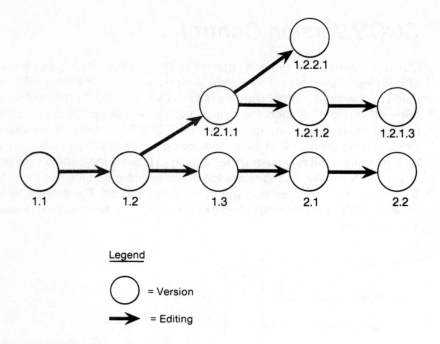

Legend

◯ = Version

➡ = Editing

Fig. 10.3. *SCCS Versions with Branching*

SCCS Management Utilities

In addition to allowing users to withdraw and resubmit files under its control, SCCS includes a number of utility functions to aid in file management. Using SCCS utilities, the user can perform the following:

- Show the differences between two versions of a file

- Print the contents of a text file, with each line showing the version number, indicating when it was most recently changed

- Automatically insert information, such as the date, the current version number, and the name of the file, when the file is printed

- Show the history of a version of an SCCS file, listing all the versions that logically precede it

- Remove the latest version of an SCCS file, reverting back to the previous version to recover from major errors.

Table 10.4 lists the SCCS utilities.

Table 10.4
SCCS Utilities

admin	Places a file under SCCS control and changes its description
get	Obtains a version of an SCCS file for examination or editing
delta	Creates a new version of an SCCS file, including new editing changes
prs	Prints parts of an SCCS file
rmdel	Removes a version of an SCCS file that was created in error
cdc	Changes the comments associated with a version of an SCCS file
what	Searches SCCS files for identified comments embedded in the text
sccsdiff	Prints the differences between versions of SCCS files
comb	Combines stored versions of SCCS files, obliterating part of the file's history
val	Validates SCCS files to ensure that they have a specified version number, etc.
unget	Notifies SCCS that a version withdrawn for editing will not be edited

Execution Profiling

Programmers concerned with the performance of their programs can use
the **time** command to obtain information about program execution times.
The command

```
$ time report1
real      35.1
user       2.1
sys        0.1
$ ▪
```

executes the **report1** program and displays the elapsed wall clock time during its execution, the CPU time spent executing the program, and the CPU
time spent within the UNIX kernel on behalf of the program.

UNIX System V includes new utilities to assist programmers in improving the performance of their programs and to aid a system administrator in improving overall system performance. Table 10.5 lists these utilities.

Table 10.5
Utilities for Execution Profiling

time	Prints execution times for a program
prof	Prints an execution profile of a program
sadp	Prints a table or histogram profiling disk activity
sar	Samples system activity over a time interval
sag	Graphs system activity over a time interval

Programmers can compile a program with a profiling option to identify the areas in the program where performance can be improved. When the program is executed, a disk file is automatically generated that records the execution flow of the program over a period of time. The **prof** utility is used to analyze this data and to determine where a program is spending the largest percentage of its execution time. These sections of the program then become prime candidates for performance improvement work.

A similar capability is available to monitor the execution of the UNIX system itself over a time interval. Utilities sample system activity and present it in tabular or graphical form for analysis. Statistics can be obtained on CPU utilization, disk buffer activity, I/O activity, system calls, swapping activity, and several other aspects of system performance. Analysis of this data may indicate the need for additional memory, disk drives, and other system resources.

Communications

UNIX includes several utilities that support system-to-system communications. Considering UNIX's origins within AT&T, it is not surprising that most of these utilities support communications through the switched telephone network. In fact, electronic communications between UNIX systems has become a very popular alternative to mail services among experienced UNIX users in universities, research laboratories, and industrial companies around the world. An entire network of interconnected UNIX systems is available, and users can often be found routing messages through two or three intermediate machines to reach their ultimate destinations.

Communications Facilities

Utilities provided with the standard UNIX system support the following communications functions:

- *Remote login.* A user on one system can login to another system across a communications link. A user may execute commands on the remote system and perform other tasks as if the user were using the system directly.

- *File transfer.* A user on one system can transfer files to and from another system across a communications link.

- *Remote job entry.* A user can prepare jobs for execution on an IBM mainframe and submit them for execution across a communications link. The mainframe sends the output back across the link, for further processing on the UNIX system.

Remote Login to a UNIX System

The **cu** (**c**all **U**NIX) utility allows a user connected on one UNIX system to login temporarily to another system. Figure 11.1 shows a typical **cu** connection. The local system may access the remote system directly over a dedicated communications line, indirectly over the public telephone network, or through a local area network (LAN) linking the systems. If the local system is equipped with an automatic dialing modem, the user can specify a telephone number with the **cu** command, for automatic dialing of the remote system.

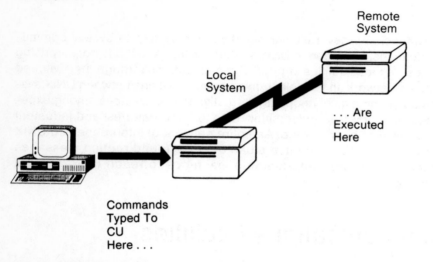

Local System

Remote System

. . . Are Executed Here

Commands Typed To CU Here . . .

Fig. 11.1. *Remote Login with CU*

Once the user is connected to the remote system, commands are entered as if the user were directly logged on to the remote system. The entered commands access the files and devices of the remote system. The **cu** utility also supports other communications capabilities with the remote system, allowing a user to perform the following tasks:

- Escape from the communications link to run a single command on the local system

- Run a command on the remote system, capturing its output on the local system

- Run a command on the local system, sending its output to the remote system
- Copy a file from the local system to the remote system
- Copy a file from the remote system to the local system

The **cu** utility can even be used to communicate with non-UNIX systems, to assist in transfer of data files, conversion of programs, and other communications functions.

Remote File Transfer

The **uucp** (**U**NIX-to-**U**NIX **c**opy) facility copies files from one UNIX system to another across a communications link. The facility is actually a family of utilities, as listed in Table 11.1.

Table 11.1
The UUCP Utilities

uucp	Copies files to and from a remote system
uuto	Copies files to a remote system
uulog	Prints information about file copy activity from a log file
uuname	Lists the names of known remote systems
uustat	Prints the status of the file copy operations, communications links, and remote systems
uupick	Selectively accepts files received from a remote system for further processing
uux	Executes commands on a remote system, routing input and output from other systems

This facility identifies a remote file by its path name on the remote system. The name of the remote system is prefixed to the path name and separated from it by an *exclamation point* (**!**). The **uucp** path name

finance!/joe/report

identifies the file named **/joe/report** on the system named **finance**. The **uucp** facility uses a configuration file, maintained by the system administrator, to determine how to access a remote system. Details of the communications network are thus hidden from ordinary users.

The **uucp** facility also supports file transfers forwarded through intermediate systems. For example, the **uucp** path name

chicago!finance!/joe/report

identifies the file **/joe/report** on the **finance** system, which is accessed by sending messages through the **chicago** system.

Using the **uucp** utilities, the user can track the progress of a file transfer and request notification by UNIX mail when the transfer is complete. A user on the remote system can also be notified. The **uucp** facility can copy files directly or copy them to a temporary spool directory, freeing the original copy of the file for further use.

The **uucp** utilities use a communications protocol that automatically detects data transmission errors. Each record transmitted includes a calculated error detection field, which is recalculated when the record is received. A discrepancy means that an error has occurred, causing retransmission of the record. This error detection technique ensures that most communications errors will be detected and automatically corrected.

In addition to the role that it plays in in-house networks, **uucp** plays an important role in linking UNIX users to one another. Over the years, a large and informal network of UNIX systems, linked by **uucp**, has emerged. Named USENET, this dial-up network links most of the major academic and research UNIX installations around the country (such as Berkeley) and also includes literally thousands of individual UNIX installations.

The store-and-forward capabilities of **uucp** allow a user on the USENET network to send electronic mail and files to any other user in the network, provided the **uucp** path to that user's system is known. The network carries an enormous amount of mail, news, memos, programming advice, and other information every day. In fact, the existence of USENET as a network to bind the UNIX development community together is an important factor in the growth of UNIX usage and popularity.

Remote Job Entry

The *Remote Job Entry* (RJE) facility allows users of a UNIX system to submit jobs for processing on an IBM mainframe. Using standard UNIX text-editing utilities, the user prepares the IBM job stream and any associated data files. Output from the mainframe, which would ordinarily be printed on the mainframe's printer or punched on the mainframe's card punch, is instead transmitted back to the UNIX system and stored in files for the user. With RJE, the user has both access to mainframe processing power for job execution and access to the wealth of UNIX utilities for preparing job input and processing job output.

The RJE facility operates as a family of background processes. The user submits a job for RJE processing with the **send** utility. The RJE facility places the job into a queue of jobs awaiting transmission and eventually transmits the job to the mainframe for processing. The mainframe then copies the submitted job into *its* input job queue and eventually schedules the job for execution. When mainframe processing is complete, the mainframe transmits job output back to the UNIX system, where the RJE facility stores the job output in a temporary file. When the transmission concludes, the user is notified, and the user may access the temporary files for further processing. Figure 11.2 summarizes RJE operation.

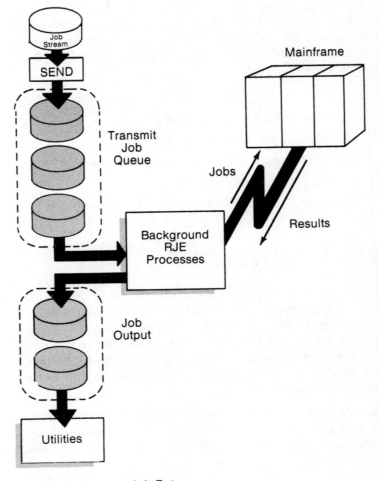

Fig. 11.2. *Remote Job Entry*

Options to the **send** utility allow a user to gather together data files for transmission, display messages and prompts on the terminal, and perform EBCDIC-to-ASCII conversion. The **send** utility also includes a full-blown macro facility for processing the job stream before transmission. The macro facility allows the user to perform the following tasks:

- Substitute text for variables

- Conditionally include or omit text

- Interactively prompt the user for variable values

Using these capabilities, an application designer can construct a mainframe job stream that includes various processing options. For example, a job stream may include options for end-of-week, end-of-month, and end-of-quarter processing. The job stream can prompt for user input and transmit the proper parts of the job stream text, based on user response. The user dialogue can thus be very simple, even though the underlying job control language may be quite complex. Table 11.2 summarizes the utilities that comprise the RJE facility.

Table 11.2
Remote Job Entry (RJE) Utilities

send	Submits job streams for mainframe execution
rjestat	Displays the status of RJE jobs submitted for execution
rjeinit	Initializes the background RJE facility
rjehalt	Terminates RJE processing

Distributed File Systems

With the growing popularity of local area networks has come an intense interest in creating more intimate connections between networked UNIX systems than simple file transfer links. PC LANs, for example, give connected PCs direct access to files on a common file server so that the systems can share file contents. Because UNIX-based systems on a LAN have local disk storage that is already shared among local users, file sharing for UNIX LANs has taken a more peer-to-peer approach.

During the last few years, several system vendors and software companies have introduced UNIX LAN file-sharing schemes. All these schemes share a common approach—the creation of a distributed file system that includes both local and remote files and provides transparent access to both. Of these schemes, two have emerged as the leading commercial implementations:

- *Remote File Sharing (RFS).* AT&T's distributed file system capability, introduced as part of UNIX System V.3. Originally available only on AT&T's STARLAN local area network, RFS is being adopted by UNIX system vendors as they sell later versions of UNIX System V.

- *Network File System (NFS™).* A distributed file-system product developed by Sun Microsystems and now licensed by more than 100 different organizations, including many UNIX systems manufacturers. Evolving out of Sun's need for a distributed file system linking its Sun workstations, NFS has become a vendor-independent de facto standard.

Remote File Sharing

The goal of AT&T's Remote File Sharing facility is to provide transparent access to remote files and other resources across a local area network. Transparent access is achieved by extending the UNIX concept of file-system mounting across system boundaries (see Chapter 4). Instead of mounting a local file system on the local root-file system, RFS allows a system manager to mount a remote directory and its subdirectory structure on the local file-system hierarchy.

Figure 11.3 shows how RFS works. The manager of the **mfg** system decides that part of the file hierarchy on that system should be accessible to others on the network. The manager advertises the availability of this subhierarchy through the RFS **adv** (**adv**ertise) command. The command also assigns the subhierarchy a *resource name*, by which it is known on the network.

The manager of the **mktg** system now can attach this resource to the local file hierarchy. First, a "dummy" directory is created in the local hierarchy at the point where the remote files should appear. Then the **mount** command is used to paste the remote resource over the dummy directory. Users on the **mktg** system now see a file hierarchy that transparently includes the remote files and directories. Users of the **mktg** system have full access to the remote files. The UNIX utilities can be used to copy, display, edit, and manipulate the files. The UNIX file-locking scheme also operates across the network (although UNIX cannot detect deadlocks caused by processes operating on two different hosts).

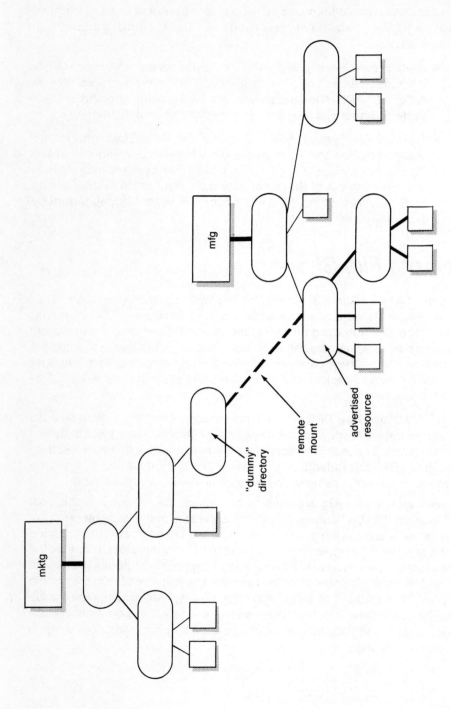

Fig. 11.3. *A Remote File Sharing Operation*

The RFS concept also allows sharing of remote devices. By mounting a remote system's **/dev** directory, system managers can provide access to remote devices and named pipes. This technique can be used, for example, to share a backup device among several different systems on a network. The users on each system can use the remote device in UNIX utility commands (such as **cpio**) as if it were a local device on their own system. Named pipe support allows interprocess communication between programs on different hosts.

For administrative purposes, hosts on an RFS network can be grouped into *domains*. Each domain has a system designated as a *name server*, which translates host and resource names in the domain to actual locations on the network. This translation allows programs and users to reference network resources symbolically, without worrying about where the resources actually reside on the network. Therefore, network topology can be changed without affecting users.

Security is always a concern when a network provides access by other systems into a system's files. RFS provides three levels of security:

- *Connection security* determines which hosts are allowed to connect to the system.

- *Resource security* restricts access to individual resources on a system. The system manager can use RFS commands to restrict each resource for access only by specific hosts. In addition, the resource can be shared in a read-only mode, allowing other systems to access but not modify local files.

- *User security* restricts the access privileges of individual users on other hosts. UNIX enforces the local UNIX security provisions for RFS access.

In addition to these three security levels, RFS provides several different options for implementing user security. With these options, the system manager can tailor security to meet requirements of the particular installation. The options include the following:

- *Special "guest" ID.* All remote access take place through a special "network-guest" user ID on the local system. The privileges of this guest-user ID determine the access permissions for all remote users.

- *Networkwide user ID's.* Remote-access permissions are determined by the remote user's user ID. This scheme requires networkwide coordination of user ID's, but it may be useful in a cooperative network.

- *Networkwide user names.* Remote-access permissions are determined by the remote user's user name. This scheme requires networkwide coordination of user names, but different user ID's can be used on the various systems.

- *User-name mapping.* Remote user names are explicitly translated into local user names, which determine access permissions. This scheme gives the system manager tight user-by-user control over remote-access permissions.

Operation of RFS is largely transparent to the UNIX system user. Table 11.3 lists the UNIX utilities that are used by the RFS user and the system manager.

Table 11.3
RFS Utilities

adv	Advertises a resource to the network
unadv	"Unadvertises" a shared resource
mount	Establishes a link to a remote resource
umount	Removes the link to a remote resource
fumount	Forces unmount of local resource by all hosts
nsquery	Lists available resources on other hosts
rmntstat	Lists mounts of resources by other hosts
fusage	Lists disk usage by other hosts
fuser	Lists users currently using resources
rfstart	Starts RFS processing
rfstop	Halts RFS processing

Network File System

Like RFS, the major goal of Sun Microsystems' Network File System (NFS) is to provide a transparent distributed file system. The two products use remarkably similar techniques for achieving this goal. Like RFS, NFS extends the UNIX **mount** command to attach a subhierarchy of a remote system over a dummy directory on the local machine. Instead of the RFS concept of resource names, the NFS **mount** command deals specifically with the remote system's directory structure. For example, to attach the remote directory **/usr/mary/reports** on the **mfg** system to the local directory **/sales/reports**, the system manager enters

```
$ mount mfg:/usr/mary/reports /sales/reports
```

Like RFS, NFS allows a system manager to restrict the parts of the local file hierarchy that are accessible to other systems. The **/etc/exports** file contains a list of accessible local directories and, optionally, a list of the host systems that are allowed to mount each directory. NFS also provides a "Yellow Pages" service, which translates network names into specific host addresses. A *Yellow Pages server* provides this name translation, and the network can be divided into domains that are served by different Yellow Pages servers.

In addition to its distributed file system, NFS provides several additional features for intersystem communications:

- *Remote Procedure Calls.* A program executing on one host can call a subprogram on another host using the NFS remote procedure call (RPC) mechanism. The remote call resembles a local procedure call and provides a simple, elegant model for implementing client/server communications. NFS automatically handles the required housekeeping, such as waking up the appropriate server on the remote machine.

- *External Data Representation.* Because NFS was conceived as a vendor-independent system, different systems on an NFS network are likely to store various types of data differently. External data representation (XDR) is a standard for passing binary data across an NFS network and is especially important in remote procedure calls. A calling program first translates its own data into XDR and then makes the call. The called program similarly translates the data from XDR into its own data formats before manipulating the data. In this way, dissimilar systems can communicate effectively in an NFS network.

- *Interprocess Communication.* NFS is based on the TCP/IP protocols, which offer a widely accepted model for interprocess communications. Pioneered in Berkeley UNIX, the TCP socket model can be used transparently by two processes, whether they are located on the same or on different host systems. NFS thus taps into the power of a well-known and widely accepted IPC mechanism.

Although RFS and NFS have their differences, both achieve the central goal of creating a usable distributed file system. If the history of the UNIX market is any indication, one of the two schemes will emerge as a de facto standard.

NFS has the advantages of having been available for a longer period of time and of enjoying support from many different vendors. NFS runs on EtherNet™ and is based on the widely used TCP/IP protocols. Sun has also enhanced NFS with auxiliary products. A PC version of NFS, PC-NFS, allows personal computers to participate in an NFS network, and Sun's X/Windows windowing package also supports NFS. Other vendors have provided NFS implementations for VAX/VMS and other important computer environments.

The main advantage of RFS is that it is an AT&T product. RFS support is already integrated into the UNIX System V source as distributed by AT&T. This factor minimizes the amount of integration required by a computer vendor. The movement of the UNIX market toward a standard based on UNIX System V thus seems to favor RFS.

The STREAMS Facility

With the introduction of UNIX System V.3, AT&T introduced a new STREAMS facility for developing UNIX communications services. The main motivation for STREAMS is the proliferation of communications protocols and standards. The OSI standards, SNA, TCP/IP, XNS, X.25, and other protocols all play significant roles in computer communications today. STREAMS provides a standard interface for character input/output on UNIX systems and gives network developers a set of tools for developing modular layered communications protocols.

STREAMS provides three main benefits:

- User-level programs can be independent of communications protocols. A user data-inquiry program based on STREAMS, for example, can run over an SDLC-based network or an X.25 link without changing the user program.

- Higher-level protocols can be independent of lower-level protocols. A TCP/IP protocol module, for example, can be used on an EtherNet LAN or a Token Ring LAN without change.

- STREAMS-based protocols are integrated with the UNIX file system. UNIX applications programs can access the data communications link through normal UNIX system calls (**open**, **close**, **read**, **write**); and the data is transparently handled by layers of protocol modules within the UNIX kernel.

Although STREAMS per se is not useful to the average UNIX user, STREAMS should have a major impact on UNIX-based communications. Because STREAMS allows effective reuse of protocol layers, it continues the UNIX tradition of "building on the work of others." The future should see a steady flow of STREAMS-based communications protocols, both from AT&T and from third-party vendors.

12

The Future of UNIX

The UNIX system today enjoys a position as the de facto standard operating system for multiuser, 16-bit, and 32-bit microcomputer systems. UNIX's influence is also being felt in the minicomputer and personal computer markets, and even the mainframe computer market. Acceptance of the UNIX system is widespread and growing. Although UNIX may not have achieved the dominance of the computer industry predicted by its most ardent supporters a few years ago, the system's influence and importance have steadily expanded.

Predicting the future of the UNIX market has become a favorite pastime among market researchers and the computer trade press. Almost all the "experts" agree that the market for UNIX-based systems will grow dramatically over the next few years. This chapter discusses the factors that will influence both the rate and direction of growth, and considers the impact of these factors on the future of the UNIX system.

UNIX Development at AT&T

With the announcement of UNIX System V in January, 1983, AT&T assumed a much more aggressive role in the development of the market for UNIX-based systems. The announcement of System V marked several "firsts" for a UNIX system from AT&T:

- The version of UNIX licensed to the "outside world" was, for the first time, the same as the version in general use within the Bell System. Previously, AT&T had only licensed UNIX versions that were as much as eighteen months behind its own current versions. Parity between the internal and external versions of UNIX, along with the breakup of AT&T, has made the Bell operating companies a large customer base for UNIX-based systems and software.

- AT&T announced, also for the first time, software support for UNIX System V. Previous UNIX versions had been licensed "as is" with no support available. The introduction of support marks a change in AT&T's role, from that of a technology licensor to that of a software supplier.

- AT&T announced that it was "locking" the UNIX system kernel in System V. Although future UNIX system versions may include kernel enhancements, AT&T has guaranteed that these versions will be upwardly compatible with the System V kernel. The specification of the System V kernel has now been formalized in the System V Interface Document (SVID). This document encourages software developers to write UNIX-based applications, confident that their software will run on future UNIX versions without modification.

In the years since the original UNIX System V announcement, AT&T has released significant revisions and upgrades to System V. These new releases have followed through on the promise of upward compatibility while providing significant new features, such as file locking, remote file sharing, improved system administration, and virtual memory. With these enhancements, AT&T has shown its willingness to adopt improvements pioneered by others, especially the enhancements of the Berkeley UNIX versions and the /usr/group standard.

Active UNIX development continues at AT&T, and the future should see a steady growth of the capabilities offered by UNIX. The pace of that development and AT&T's commitment to maintaining the UNIX System V standard cast serious doubts on the prospects of proprietary UNIX extensions and enhancements.

UNIX and the Minicomputer Suppliers

The impact of UNIX-based microcomputers has been felt by the traditional minicomputer suppliers, and they have responded with UNIX-based offerings of their own. Digital Equipment's ULTRIX operating system for the VAX system family is derived from Berkeley UNIX, and the original Berkeley software remains popular on VAX systems. DEC's major sales thrust still supports its proprietary operating systems, however, and a question remains of whether DEC's support of UNIX is in name only.

Data General offers two UNIX versions on its Eclipse™ family of minis and superminis. One DG offering is a native mode UNIX port. The other offering is implemented as an extension to DG's own AOS™ operating system and, as a result, suffers from a lack of complete compatibility with standard UNIX. The DG approach illustrates the dilemma of the minicomputer manufacturers. Their large installed bases force them to maintain compatibility with their own proprietary systems, yet the emerging market power of the UNIX system forces a response from them as well. The result is often an unhappy compromise.

Hewlett-Packard offers UNIX on the entire product line of HP 9000 systems. At the low end, the HP 9000 series includes engineering workstations and small multiuser systems. At the high end, the family includes supermini systems based on a reduced instruction set (RISC) design. Hewlett-Packard has signaled clearly its intention to use UNIX as one of its two standard operating systems. The other operating system, MPE, continues to be HP's focus in the commercial market. Like Data General, HP faces the problems of entering the UNIX market while preserving compatibility for thousands of installed customers, who represent the majority of HP's sales.

The Move to Standardization

In the mid-1980s, the key controversy in the UNIX market was over the proliferation of UNIX versions and the lack of a single standard version of UNIX. Although different versions still exist, the controversy is largely over. The marketplace is rapidly standardizing on UNIX System V, the de facto UNIX standard.

The power of the System V standard is evidenced by the efforts to bring the two major alternative UNIX versions—Berkeley UNIX and XENIX—into compliance with System V. Sun Microsystems and AT&T have announced a joint project to produce a "merged UNIX," which will remove incompatibilities between the Berkeley version and System V. This project has produced a document describing and characterizing these incompatibilities and an overall game plan for removing them. Where absolute incompatibilities exist, the direction is likely to be to bend the Berkeley implementation into compatibility with System V.

On the XENIX front, Microsoft and AT&T made an agreement early in 1987, to produce a XENIX System V version that would comply with AT&T's System V Interface Definition. As part of this agreement, Microsoft received the right to use the name *UNIX* to apply to the new XENIX version. This occasion marks the first time that AT&T has ever licensed the UNIX trademark to another company. This act is a recognition of the market power that Microsoft enjoys, not only as the vendor of the most widely installed UNIX version but also as the supplier of MS-DOS and IBM's new OS/2.

While work proceeds on merging the "real world" standards for UNIX, AT&T has also continued its formal specification of UNIX. The *System V Interface Definition* (SVID) has been revised twice since its first appearance, mainly with the addition of optional standard features that reflect actual features in AT&T System V. In parallel with the Interface Definition, AT&T has offered the *System V Verification Suite* (SVVS), a family of tests that checks an operating system's compatibility with the SVID definition.

Standards efforts have proceeded at a rapid pace outside AT&T as well. The UNIX user's group, IEEE, the International Standards Organization, the National Bureau of Standards, and X/OPEN (an international consortium of computer vendors) are all actively developing specifications for UNIX compatibility. The POSIX standard from IEEE, which forms the basis for all these efforts, was published in April, 1986, and seems assured of formal international standard status.

These practical and informal standardization efforts are all driving toward the common goal of establishing for UNIX a common standard that will increase applications portability and standardization. Although real differences still exist in various UNIX implementations, the direction clearly is toward convergence rather than divergence.

UNIX, MS-DOS, and OS/2

The UNIX operating system has become both a competitor to other microcomputer operating systems and a source of inspiration for their continuing development. UNIX-like features have appeared in MS-DOS over the years, including the UNIX hierarchical file system, input/output redirection, pipes, and UNIX-like system calls. UNIX also has had a strong influence on the multitasking capabilities provided by MS-Windows, which form the foundation for multitasking under IBM's new OS/2 personal-computer operating system as well.

Microsoft's new OS/2 operating system has adopted another UNIX characteristic with its attempt to enforce a high-level system call interface and eliminate direct hardware access. The portability benefits provided by this high-level interface have been well demonstrated by UNIX. They also have direct application in the personal computer market, where they can insulate applications from underlying advances in PC technology. The challenge faced by OS/2 is to provide a system call interface with enough capability and performance to support the kind of application responsiveness to which PC users are accustomed.

UNIX and the Intel 80386

The opportunity for UNIX-based systems has expanded dramatically with the availability of the Intel 80386, a 32-bit microprocessor that is compatible with the Intel processors which power the IBM PC family. The 80386 offers, for the first time in the Intel product line, a microprocessor with built-in hardware features that support the needs of an operating system like UNIX. These features include hardware protection, on-board memory management, well-defined supervisor and user states, and expanded addressing that supports literally gigabytes of main memory.

The 80386 is widely viewed as an ideal vehicle for implementing UNIX on a microprocessor, and the market will see a proliferation of systems based on the 80386. In addition to its architectural features, the 80386 features a high level of performance, allowing system vendors to build microprocessor-based systems with performance well into the traditional minicomputer range. The 80386 will find its way into many different kinds of computer systems, including

- High-performance personal computers
- Multiuser small-business systems
- File and database servers for PC-LANs

The dominant operating systems in the first category will certainly be MS-DOS and OS/2. UNIX seems assured of a major role in the second category. The operating system of choice for the third category remains an open question.

The 80386 provides another interesting opportunity for UNIX as a host operating system for multiple MS-DOS users. Several vendors have already introduced for the 80386 an operating system that effectively shares the processor among multiple MS-DOS sessions. The user of the 80386 system thus gets the benefits of working in parallel with multiple MS-DOS applications (such as 1-2-3, WordPerfect®, and dBASE®). Some of these "hypervisors" are based on UNIX, and others are based on proprietary technology. Whether these hybrid UNIX/DOS systems become important or just fill the gap until OS/2 is widely available is another open question.

Key Market Segments

An important development in the UNIX market has been the emergence of key market segments and key customers that have created volume demand for UNIX-based systems, software, and services. Purchases by these segments and customers continue to provide the fuel that drives the UNIX market.

- *Engineering workstations* are perhaps the most significant UNIX market because they are the segment where UNIX has most clearly established its dominance. All indications are that UNIX will continue to dominate this segment, which should continue to grow as the entry price for powerful workstations drops dramatically. The UNIX-based Apple Macintosh and Sun workstations priced below $5,000 are just two examples of this trend.

- *Multiuser engineering systems* continue to be a UNIX stronghold. The popularity of UNIX on Digital's VAX systems has created a flurry of UNIX activity in the engineering minicomputer market, with UNIX offerings from HP, DG, Wang, Prime, and others. Again, all the signs point to continued UNIX dominance in this segment.

- *Software development* remains a major application of UNIX, and machines sold for software development may comprise as much as 20 percent of the UNIX systems market. The systems used in this segment range from large, multiuser VAX installations to individual workstations with custom-software development tools. A significant number of CASE (Computer-Aided Software Engineering) tools now run on UNIX-based workstations, indicating that UNIX may emerge as an important cross-development environment for mainframe applications as well.

- *Small business systems* have emerged as an important market segment for UNIX systems, characterized by systems from Altos, NCR, and AT&T. UNIX is the only operating system standard in this segment, but UNIX is far from playing a dominant role. The proprietary operating systems on business minicomputers from IBM, DEC, HP,

DG, Wang, and others have large installed bases and loyal follow-ings; and this market segment continues to be fragmented with no discernible motion toward a standard.

- *The Federal government* is the single largest source of volume UNIX system purchases. UNIX provides a way for Federal agencies to preserve applications compatibility despite the multivendor computer installations that inevitably result from government procurement practices. As a result, UNIX is now specified as mandatory on a majority of Federal computer procurements.

- *The Bell operating companies* are another major source of UNIX system purchases. A great deal of UNIX expertise is found within these companies, and their sheer size means they have a large amount of computer-purchasing power. In addition, many operating companies are launching new ventures to sell data-processing equipment including UNIX-based systems.

The continued health and prosperity of these key UNIX markets is one of the main factors in the future success of UNIX.

The Role of IBM

No single factor has a larger potential impact on the market for UNIX-based systems than the actions of IBM. IBM has introduced versions of UNIX on several products, including

- IX/370, a version of UNIX that runs on IBM mainframe systems

- XENIX for the IBM PC

- The IBM PC/RT, a UNIX-based engineering workstation

Despite these introductions, UNIX does not appear to play a strategic role in IBM's product plans. Rather, IBM has offered UNIX as a way to satisfy customer requirements or as a way to enter a market where UNIX is an established standard, like the PC/RT.

UNIX has emerged as the "alternative operating system," one espoused by the "other" computer manufacturers who compete with IBM. For these other vendors, UNIX offers the appeal of vendor independence and a unifying force that can provide compatibility through an entire product line. Notably, the lack of that kind of compatibility is precisely what is cited as the most glaring weakness of IBM's computer offerings.

IBM's announced Systems Application Architecture (SAA) is a bold plan to bring together IBM's product families in critical areas, such as user interface, communications, and database management. The result, says IBM, will be enhanced portability for applications throughout the IBM product line. Unsaid, but clearly implied, is that such portability would make IBM an even more dominant competitor in the computer business. If the SAA strategy is successful, other computer vendors may find themselves explaining how their products fit into SAA rather than how their products provide a superior alternative to IBM.

The success of UNIX thus depends, to a certain extent, on IBM's success with its SAA strategy and the speed with which it is implemented. In any case, UNIX seems destined to play the role of an alternative operating-system standard. UNIX will continue to serve as a rallying point for computer system vendors, software suppliers, and major customers who seek power and portability for multiuser data processing.

Appendix

System Calls for UNIX System V

File and Device Input/Output

open	Open a file for input/output
close	Conclude input/output to a file
read	Read data from a file
write	Write data to a file
lseek	Move file pointer in file
ioctl	Device control operations
fcntl	File control and locking operations
fstat	Get file status information
dup	Duplicate file descriptor
chdir	Change working directory
chroot	Change to a different root directory

File Creation, Status, and Security

creat	Create a new file
mknod	Create a directory or special file
link	Create a new link to a file
unlink	Remove a link to a file

access	Get file access permissions
chmod	Change file access permissions
chown	Change the owner of a file
utime	Change file access/modification times
stat	Get file status
umask	Set/get file creation mask
mount	Mount a file system
umount	Unmount a file system
ustat	Get file system statistics
mkdir	Create a directory
rmdir	Delete a directory
getdents	Read directory entries from a directory
access	Determine access permission for a file
statfs	Get information about a file system
fstatfs	Get information about a file system
sysfs	Get information about file system types

Process Control

exec	Execute a new program
pause	Suspend process, awaiting a signal
alarm	Set process alarm clock
exit	Terminate process
fork	Start a child process
wait	Await termination of child process
kill	Terminate or send signal to a process
signal	Specify action in response to signal
sigset	Set system action for signals
sighold	Defer signal during critical code section
sigrelse	Re-enable signal after sighold
sigignore	Set system to ignore a signal
sigpause	Pause until signal is received
nice	Change process priority

Process Status

getpid	Get process ID number
getppid	Get parent process ID number
setpgrp	Set the process group ID number
getpgrp	Get process group ID number
setuid	Set user ID number
getuid	Get user ID number

setgid	Set group ID number
getgid	Get group ID number
geteuid	Get effective user ID number
getegid	Get effective group ID number
times	Get process execution time information
ulimit	Get and set process limits
brk	Request additional main memory
sbrk	Request additional main memory
plock	Lock a process in main memory

Interprocess Communications and Synchronization

pipe	Create a pipe
msgget	Get an IPC message queue for use
msgop	Send/receive messages through an IPC message queue
msgctl	Control an IPC message queue
semget	Get a set of semaphores for use
semop	Perform operations on a semaphore
semctl	Control a semaphore
maus	Access shared memory
shmget	Get shared memory for use
shmop	Attach to shared memory
shmctl	Control shared memory

Miscellaneous

acct	Enable/disable accounting
profil	Enable/disable executing profiling
ptrace	Trace execution of child process
stime	Set time and date
time	Get time of day
sync	Flush kernel file buffers
uname	Get name of current UNIX system
getmsg	Get a STREAMS message
putmsg	Send a STREAMS message
poll	Check status of a STREAMS file

Appendix

Utilities in UNIX System V

accept	Permits spooling requests for a printer
acctcom	Searches and prints accounting files
adb	Absolute debugger
admin	Creates and administers SCCS files
adv	Permits remote access to a resource
ar	Maintains portable archives
as	Assembler
asa	Interprets ASA carriage control characters
assist	Helps a user learn shell commands
at	Executes commands at a later time
awk	Pattern scanning and processing language
banner	Makes banners
basename	Outputs the file name from a path name
basic	A BASIC interpreter
batch	Executes commands when system load permits
bc	Desktop calculator with programming constructs
bdiff	Compares two large files
bfs	Scans big files
bs	A compiler/interpreter
cal	Outputs a calendar
calendar	Appointment scheduler
cancel	Cancels a previous spooling request

cat	Concatenates and prints files
cb	Formats C programs
cc	C language compiler
cd	Changes the current working directory
cdc	Changes comments for an SCCS delta
cflow	Generates flow graphs
chgrp	Changes group ownership of a file
chmod	Changes file access permissions
chown	Changes ownership of a file
chroot	Changes file system root for a command
ckbupsed	Lists file systems scheduled for backup
cmp	Compares two files
cmpress	Reorganizes a file system to reduce fragmentation
col	Filters reverse line feeds
comb	Combines SCCS deltas
comm	Selects or rejects lines common to two sorted files
convert	Converts formats of object and archive files
cp	Copies files
cpio	Copies file archives
cpp	C language preprocessor
crash	Displays formatted system dump information
crypt	Encodes and decodes files
csplit	Splits files based on pattern matching
ct	Spawns a getty process to a remote terminal
ctrace	Traces C program execution
cu	Calls another UNIX system
cut	Selects columns from a tabular file
cw	Prepares constant-width text for troff
cxref	Generates C program cross-reference listing
date	Sets and prints the date
dc	Desktop calculator
dcopy	Reorganizes a file system for improved performance
dd	Performs file transformations
delta	Makes a change to an SCCS file
deroff	Removes formatting commands from a file
df	Displays free space in file system
diff	Compares two files
diff3	Compares three files
diffmk	Marks the differences between files
dircmp	Compares file contents in two directories
dirname	Outputs the path from a path name
dis	Object file disassembler
disable	Disables spooling on a printer

dname	Displays and sets domain and network names
du	Summarizes disk usage
dump	Dumps selected parts of an object file
echo	Echoes arguments
ed	Line-oriented text editor
edit	Variant of **ex** for casual users
efl	An extended FORTRAN language compiler
enable	Enables spooling on a printer
env	Executes a command in a specified environment
eqn	Mathematical equation formatter
ex	A text editor
expr	Evaluates expressions
f77	FORTRAN compiler
factor	Factors a number
false	Returns a false value
ff	Lists file name and inode information
file	Determines file type
finc	Fast incremental backup utility
find	Searches for files
frec	Recovers backups produced by **finc** or **volcopy**
fsdb	Debugs damaged file systems
fsplit	Splits FORTRAN source files
fumount	Forces unmount of an RFS resource
fusage	Displays information on RFS file usage
fuser	Lists current users of a file or RFS resource
gath	Gathers files for RJE execution
ged	Graphics editor
get	Gets a version of an SCCS file
getopt	Parses command options (obsolete)
getopts	Parses command line options
glossary	Displays definitions of technical terms
graph	Draws a graph
graphics	Accesses graphical and numerical commands
grep	Selects lines of a file based on pattern matching
grpck	Checks group file integrity
gutil	Graphical utilities
help	Provides on-line help on commands
helpadm	Modifies on-line help information
hyphen	Finds hyphenated words
id	Outputs user and group id's and names
idload	Creates user translation tables for RFS
infocmp	Lists or compares **terminfo** descriptions
install	Installs a file in a directory

ipcrm	Removes message queue, shared memory, or semaphore
ipcs	Reports interprocess communication status
join	Joins two tabular data files
kill	Terminates or signals processes
labelit	Labels a file system
ld	Link editor
lex	Generates lexical analysis routines
line	Copies a line from standard input to output
lint	C language syntax checker
list	Lists C programs with line numbers
ln	Links file names
locate	Suggests UNIX commands based on keywords
login	Admits authorized user to a system
logname	Outputs the user's login name
lorder	Finds the ordering relation for an object library
lp	Line printer spooler
lpadmin	Configures the **lp** spooling system
lpr	Line printer spooler
lpstat	Prints spooling status information
ls	Lists contents of directories
m4	Macro processor
mail	Sends and receives UNIX mail
mailx	Extended UNIX mail facility
make	Regenerates groups of programs
makekey	Generates an encryption key
man	Prints on-line manual entries
mesg	Permits or denies messages
mkdir	Makes a directory
mkfs	Creates a file system on a disk
mknod	Creates directory entry for a special file
mkshlib	Creates a shared library
mm	Text-formatting macros
mmt	Typesetting macros
mount	Mounts a file system
mv	Moves files
mvdir	Moves a directory
newform	Reformats lines of a text file
newgrp	Changes active group membership
news	Prints news items
nice	Runs a program at reduced priority
nl	Line-numbering filter
nm	Prints names from a common object file

nohup	Runs a program immune from hang-ups and quits
nroff	Text formatter
nsquery	Displays information about available RFS resources
od	Outputs an octal dump of a file
pack	Packs files
passwd	Changes a user's password
paste	Merges lines of files
pcat	Concatenates packed files
pcc	Portable C compiler
pg	Browses file contents on a terminal screen
pr	Prints files
prof	Outputs execution profile data
prs	Prints an SCCS file
ps	Outputs process status
ptx	Generates a permuted index
pwck	Checks password file integrity
pwd	Prints the name of the current working directory
ratfor	Preprocessor for rational FORTRAN dialect
regcmp	Regular expression compiler
reject	Disallows spooling requests for a printer
rfadmin	Adds and removes hosts from an RFS domain
rfpasswd	Sets host passwords for RFS
rfstart	Starts RFS operation
rfstop	Halts RFS operation
rjestat	Outputs RJE status
rm	Removes file names
rmdel	Removes an SCCS delta
rmdir	Removes directories
rmntstat	Displays status of RFS resources
rsh	Restricted UNIX system shell
sact	Prints current SCCS editing activity
sadp	Outputs disk access profile data
sag	Outputs a system activity graph
sar	Outputs a system activity report
scat	Concatenates and prints files
sccsdiff	Compares two versions of an SCCS file
sdb	Symbolic debugger
sdiff	Compares two files
se	Screen editor
sed	Stream editor
send	Submits RJE jobs for execution
sh	The UNIX system shell
shl	Shell layer manager

shutdown	Shuts down the system
size	Prints the sizes of object files
sleep	Suspends execution for a time interval
sno	SNOBOL interpreter
sort	Sorts and merges files
spell	Finds spelling errors
spline	Interpolates smooth curves
split	Splits a file
starter	Displays UNIX information for new users
stat	Statistical network for graphics
strip	Removes symbol table information from an object file
stty	Sets terminal characteristics
su	Temporarily changes user ID
sum	Outputs checksum and block count for a file
sync	Writes disk buffers to disk
sysadm	Menu-driven system administration utility
tabs	Sets tabs on a terminal
tail	Outputs the last part of a file
tar	Tape file archiving
tbl	Table formatter
tee	Pipe fitter
test	Evaluates conditions
tic	Compiles **terminfo** descriptions
time	Times command execution
timex	Times command execution
toc	Generates graphical table of contents
touch	Updates access and modification times of a file
tplot	Graphics filters
tput	Queries **terminfo** database
tr	Character translation filter
troff	Phototypesetter text formatter
true	Returns a true value
tsort	Topological sort
tty	Outputs the name of a terminal
umask	Sets file creation mode mask
umount	Dismounts a file system
unadv	Disallows access to an RFS resource
uname	Outputs the name of the current UNIX system
unget	Ungets an SCCS file
uniq	Outputs a file with unique lines
units	Performs units conversions
unpack	Unpacks packed files
usage	Displays information about command usage

uucp	Copies files between UNIX systems
uulog	Outputs uucp log information
uuname	Outputs uucp names of known systems
uupick	Retrieves files sent by **uuto**
uustat	Outputs uucp status information
uuto	Copies files between UNIX systems
uux	Executes a command on a remote UNIX system
val	Validates SCCS files
vc	Version control
vi	A full-screen text editor
volcopy	Makes a raw copy of a file system
wait	Waits for completion of background processes
wall	Sends a message to all users
wc	Outputs line, word, and character counts for a file
what	Identifies SCCS files
who	Outputs information on current users
whodo	Shows who is doing what on the system
write	Sends messages to another user
xargs	Constructs an argument list and executes a command
yacc	A compiler-generating tool

Index

T

C Programmer's Toolkit
by Jack Purdum, Ph.D.

Ready-to-run subroutines highlight this task-oriented book/disk set for intermediate to advanced level programmers. Presents useful functions not found in an ANSI standard library and shows you how to design library functions. A code-intensive text!

Order #992
$39.95 USA
0-88022-457-6, 500 pp.

C Programming Guide, 3rd Edition
by Jack Purdum, Ph.D.

Hands-on practice sessions lead you step-by-step through the fundamentals of C programming. This Que classic features useful information on the ANSI C standard, common C commands, and proper syntax. A valuable resource!

Order #850
$24.95 USA
0-88022-356-1, 456 pp.

Managing Your Hard Disk, 2nd Edition
by Don Berliner

Learn the most efficient techniques for organizing the programs and data on your hard disk! This hard-working text includes management tips, essential DOS commands, an explanation of new application and utility software, and an introduction to PS/2 hardware.

Order #837
$22.95 USA
0-88022-348-0, 600 pp.

Using Assembly Language
by Allen Wyatt

Look to Que's *Using Assembly Language* for thorough coverage of all assembly language concepts! This text explains how to develop, manage, and debug subroutines; access BIOS and DOS services; and interface assembly language with Pascal, C, and BASIC.

Order #107
$24.95 USA
0-88022-297-2, 746 pp.

More Computer Knowledge from Que